Maybe You Sh[...]

Write

A Magazine!

A Complete Guide:
How to Write, Lay out, Publish and Profit
From Your Own Regional
Special-Interest Magazines

William Cory

See page 154 for a special offer on the WriteAMagazine CD ... with over 150 files and tools created from the author's 20 years of experience (that's 20 years of profit from every edition in five states).

Get Started Right!

Don't reinvent the wheel ...

Maybe You Should Write A Magazine

ISBN 9780972956796

is published by

Niche Publishing Co.

William Cory

12160 Mt. Baldy Drive

Colorado Springs. CO 80921

email: WriteAMagazine@gmail.com

CONTENTS

INTRODUCTION TO THE
REVISED EDITION

In the fifteen of years since I published the first edition of this book, everything has changed.

The skills of mechanical layout and paste up became unnecessary for anyone entering college after the year 2000; computers took over.

Sending a 4-color Matchprint along with a set of Color Separation negatives after 2002, no longer needed: Printing companies caught up with the new technologies.

Spec'ing type to be set from typed copy; it was made moot in the mid 1990's by the most elementary word processing programs.

Sending positive art, "art on a board, camera ready," was no longer done after 2004. It was either scanned and digitized, or created as a digital original.

In short, *everything* changed regarding the creation and production of all kinds of publications.

It's all digital, and it's much, much easier!

All the current digital procedures are covered in this revised edition.

The principles of the writing, marketing, organizational steps, and sales have not changed. They are also all covered here.

And, if you decide to go forward with a regional magazine of your own, the CD, Layout & Design, has also been completely updated.

I hope this and the CD will help you to create your own regional magazine, earn and extra income, and to be greatly successful!

Bill Cory
June, 2009

FOREWORD

This book is not about publishing a magazine like *Time, People, Fortune, Sports Illustrated* or *Modern Bride.*

It's about creating and publishing, on a small but *profitable* scale, your own regionally distributed magazines that will succeed on every level, financial and otherwise. As I did as a part-time freelance writer, any writer who can do research can create and publish one or more of these small but profitable special-interest publications. They not only pay for themselves, with little monetary investment required to start up (beyond standard computer equipment); they also reach the street having left a decent profit in the writer/publisher's pocket. And the profit starts with the first edition.

That's rare, I know—but that's what this book is about.

One night in 1989, lying in bed waiting for my 3-year-old son to decide to quit fussing and go to sleep, it dawned on me that there were no local magazines for Brides and Grooms. I was a wedding photographer and writer. I had been asked "every question in the book" by brides, moms of brides, sisters of brides, and a few grooms. After several years in the business, I knew all the questions they asked—and the answers to them.

That night, I decided I would write and publish a local magazine on the subject. So, with no testing, no focus groups, no investors—just a Macintosh Plus (all 8 megahertz and 1Mb RAM of it, with a monotone 9-inch screen), and the knowledge in my head—I wrote and laid out my first edition. That first edition was published three months later; it changed many aspects of my life. That was a watershed year—much more so than I realized at the time. The magazine rocketed my business from 22 weddings a year to 62 the first year, not even counting over 40 I had to turn down and refer to other photographers. Twenty years later, it has also become my family's main source of income—a source that leaves me time to do other writing and business development, and to enjoy recreation and family time. It has *almost* satisfied my "need to create," something to which all writers can relate.

Back in 1977, a man named Ralph Daigh, published a book named *Maybe You Should Write A Book.* Hence my title. But, you don't "write" a magazine, do you? Well, actually, you *can.* A "magazine," according to the accepted definition, is a collection of articles, some illustrated, normally bound in soft cover and published at regular intervals—usually quarterly or more often.

In this case, the definition still fits, with a couple of slight differences: In these magazines, the "collection of articles" is written by one person, like the chapters of a book would be. In fact, its text could be released as a book. But as a book, it would not be economically feasible. Bound as a magazine, with advertising, it's not only feasible—it's actually profitable for the publisher, effective for the advertisers, and helpful to its readers! Could you ask more from a publication?

Back in 1994, I wrote the first edition of this book. (See the cover illustrated at the top of the chapter.) I have a copy of the Docutech print version sitting beside me, *completely* different from this edition. It was so because the entire publishing process described in it has changed. Compared to this eBook, it was longer, bigger, and couldn't be published in any economical way. Now, as an eBook, it can be. And, with POD (Print On Demand) printing, it can now be made available in print. This is an almost entirely different book, especially regarding graphics and production techniques.

In 1994, I was still doing mechanical paste-up to produce my magazines. The process was complicated, difficult and time consuming. Oh, sure, I used a page layout program (PageMaker 6), but that was pretty much where the computer's involvement ended.

Back then, printers used a "process camera." ("What's that?" I hear people asking.) It is a large camera that shoots a single full-size lithographic negative of the pasted-up page, minus photos, full-page size. Then, photos (and anything else that isn't a solid single color) are shot separately, "stripped in" (taped) to the negative, and the whole negative is then exposed onto a thin metal plate with a photosensitive surface. When the plate is developed, it is a positive image with various grooves and indents where ink will be trapped. That curved plate is put into the printing press, on a large roller. As it rotates, it picks up ink in one place, and deposits the ink in a negative image onto a rubber blanket on another roller, which in turn redeposits the ink onto the paper as a positive image again. Photos in my early publications had to be black-and-white, and an 8x10, for example, that was to be reproduced at 3x4 had to be spec'ed for reduction percentage, so the printer could shoot it and make a halftone (dot-patterned negative) for it, to strip-in to the larger page negative. On and on it went: A highly detailed, hands-on, technical process. Until 1997, I didn't use a scanner, Photoshop or Illustrator to create or enhance art. The internet and email didn't exist in a usable configuration, so I couldn't receive a digital file over the Internet.

The levels of knowledge and experience with paste up needed back then to put together a decent magazine were much higher than they are now. Back then, the preparation of one 88-page edition for the printer took me four weeks of paste up, spec'ing photos, etc.

If you've been there (doing paste up, that is) you know how the basic procedures, like simply getting lines straight on the page, were time consuming, exacting, sometimes frustrating.

I had had training in some of it, but just exposure to most of it, as a staff writer at the Automobile Club of Southern California in the mid-1970's. Back then, we still had publications set in hot type and printed on running galleys from our typed copy. Desktop computers and scanners didn't exist. This eBook *obviously* couldn't have been published!

Back then, I would have never dreamed that I could, "all by myself," turn out one quality magazine, much less the seven editions per year I've done in recent years.

Now, it's actually not difficult. A writer, in particular, can easily put together a nice publication: This is so partly because the creation of text, or content, which should be the writer's specialty, is now the most demanding part of the whole project. The rest is all technical stuff that can easily be learned.

With the advent of the internet and progressively higher-speed transmission, I've produced up to nine separate editions, taking about three weeks for each "small" issue (about 40 pages) and about five to six weeks for my flagship edition, which is just over 100 pages.

The WriteAMagazine CD

You *can* publish one of these magazines and earn a profit at it. I sincerely believe that the information in this book, coupled with your own talent, skill, intelligence, experience, and diligence, will make it possible for you.

And, my WriteAMagazine CD, if ou use it, will make it happen for you much, much faster than if you start with blank pages.

See page 154 for more information, or send me an email with specific questions: WriteAMagazine@gmail.com

Order it by going to the website: **http://www.WriteAMagazine.com**.

Chapter 1

ARE YOU A WRITER, OR MAYBE A GRAPHIC ARTIST?

If you are a writer—freelance, staff or "between projects," you can create one or more publications that will generate a reliable income.

If you are a computer-based Graphic Artist, anxious to quickly build a consistent base of clients, you can do the same.

If you are *both* a writer and graphic artist, you're practically in business, and you can look forward to an income base that will allow you to pursue your heartfelt projects. (Because this business gives you supporting income, and time, to do it!)

This little publishing business has done this for me, and it can do it for you, too.

Our 2003 Central Coast Edition: 88 pages with 24 pages of color, and 145 advertisers: 115 of them were five or six-year repeaters.

Information Is Money

Everybody knows that this is the "Information Age." Those who are earning lots of money these days are those who have information to share—information that other people want and need. Information that will improve their lives. Never before has there been so *much* published, in the form of internet websites and blogs (*too* many blogs!), magazines, newspapers, books, videotapes, audiotapes and movies, in all of their forms, lengths and formats. Yet, the public is still hungry for more information.

One of the best examples is dieting. At the top of the non-fiction best seller lists every year are books on dieting, improving your body, your looks and your health—all at the same time. Some of them contain breakthrough information; most don't. Most of them are just repackaged. You'd think people had enough information on that subject. But, selling the information is still profitable because people want *new* information.

You Are Your Audience

The last time you were going to do something new, what did you look for first?

• *Information*—on whom you should hire *locally*.

The last time something unexpected happened in your home, like a garbage disposer not working or a pipe leaking, what did you look for?

• *Information*—on how to fix it or hire someone *locally*.

And, after you fixed the immediate problem, what did you look for to keep it from happening again?

• *Information*—on how to prevent it.

When you wanted to do a home improvement, like installing an automatic drip watering system for shrubs and trees, what did you seek first?

• *Information*—on how to plan and install it, or have it installed by a *local* person.

When your daughter got engaged, what did *you* look for?

• *Information*—on how to help her save (your) money on her wedding, and to help her hire the right *local* people.

Anytime we're attempting to do something new, we *always* look for information. Information that meets people's needs is always in demand, in every time, in every place, and in every medium.

And, along with the information, there will be advertising. The two go together like toast and jam.

As I write this, I'm sitting in front of a magazine stand at a Barnes & Noble Bookstore. I can see more than 1,000 magazines. Most of them are of national scope. Some are state-wide, covering "Colorado Log Homes," and "Colorado Home Decorating," etc.

What is missing? *Local* magazines!

But, what is the one characteristic shared by almost every person who walks through this store's front door? They are *local* people. Their need for information and assistance is, more often than not, a need for someone *local* who can advise them or perform a task for them.

Do they need general information on subjects covered by those national magazines? *Probably.* Would they prefer local information on the same subjects? *Definitely!*

I'll use my own business as an example.

I publish a little regional magazine titled, "Wedding & Party Magazine." If you have ever looked at a magazine stand, you might have noticed that there are well over a dozen magazines for brides. The point is this: There is no lack of wedding planning information for brides, grooms and their families. *But, most are national in scope.*

Yet, my little magazines, in every location, are always filled with advertisers—*local* advertisers—who know that their primary market is *local and regional.* They know that they can't reach that market through the national magazines. (Oh, maybe they could *reach* the market, but they'd spend so much doing it that they would go broke!) Why would they want to advertise to the whole nation or state, when over 90% of their business comes from within fifty miles?

I started in 1991. I was a so-so freelance writer, not very good at writing fiction (darn it), but not bad

I created the first edition in my garage—28 pages plus cover. It took the local wedding community by storm; my own photography bookings increased almost 300% in one year.

at explaining things. I owned a Macintosh Plus computer—just 8 megaHertz, with a 9-inch black-and-white screen. With it, I started my own publishing business. There was a need, and I filled it. There is still a need in your city, too—for information on many, many subjects that will lead readers to local service and product providers. Think about this: If the need didn't exist, the Yellow Pages wouldn't exist, either!

Every business, just like those who advertise every year in my wedding planning magazines, wants to reach its primary market. For most of the businesses in your town, that market is *local*—not national!

Imagine that you own a small business, The Home Decorating Shop. You could advertise in a publication (maybe titled: *Your New Home)* targeted toward home buyers, people who had either bought a previously owned house or had bought a newly built one. This publication offers objective information on various decorating choices, along with other information for new homeowners about cleaning, cooking, preventing leaks, winterizing, painting, upkeep, yard installation and care, and all the other things that go along with moving into a new or a previously owned house. And, imagine that the publication was free, and was distributed by all of the businesses that offered various services to home buyers, so that your money wasn't wasted on folks who weren't interested.

Finally, imagine that this was a glossy, quality publication with advertising rates that cost less per year than three months of a small display ad in the yellow phone book?

That publication is not a pipe dream. Actually, it's the general description of the magazines I have published for 20 years.

This book will teach you how to produce for that local advertiser and all the others like him or her the kind of publication I've described—one that offers quality, information, a target-market readership, and value. And, something that most businesspeople have given up on ever finding: Advertising that is *really* worth what they pay for it.

One more thing. Did I mention the *other* benefits of this part-time publishing business? I'm not much of a businessman or promoter, yet my business has prospered just because I offer a quality product that serves the needs of both advertisers and readers. Your results can be even better, especially if you have some business talent!

Still, my results are acceptable: This is my only job, and I do it only at home. It has paid for a new house. I never have to sell ad space or anything else; I just write and lay out magazines on my computer. I have time to spend with my wife, son and daughter, and time to explore and work on other writing projects (like this book), and other newly discovered interests (like building guitars)!

Have fun! --- Bill

Yup, that's me, building the guitar that my daughter is shown playing at right.

It's a different pursuit, and one that lets me use a different part of my mind. Of course, being a writer, I write on that subject, too!

Want to know more about building your own acoustic guitar? Go to:

www.KitGuitarManuals.com

Chapter 2

WHAT DO YOU KNOW?

You Probably Know Something
That Others Want To Learn About

Each of us has specialized knowledge. We each know about subjects that other people don't know about. In my case, it was weddings. I was a wedding and portrait photographer until 1992, when I photographed my last wedding. Back in 1991, after ten years as a photographer, I published the first edition of my first regional magazine, named "Wedding & Party Services Magazine."

Since then, I've increased the size of that magazine, and I've added other editions. I keep in touch with the world of weddings through various local organizations, individuals who work as independent contractor sales reps for my company, and advertisers in the magazines.

Maybe you know about weddings, too, in the broad sense that would allow you to assemble information on them? Brides want that information on a local basis, and advertisers want to reach out to those Brides while they're reading your magazine.

Or, maybe you know something about real estate, crime prevention, health, dieting, tourism, buying a house, selling a house, fixing a car, teaching a child, having a baby, or any of hundreds of other subjects. One of these—something in which you're experienced or knowledgeable—can help you launch your first magazine. (Or maybe you know of nothing on which you could publish, but you know other people who *do* know things ... well, that can work, too!)

If you are a writer, you can do research through other people and various sources. If you're a graphic artist, you can find someone who writes and collaborate with them. If you are a salesperson and organizer, find an expert in something, find someone to write about it for you, and put a project together.

Profitable Subjects

As you would guess, some subjects are better than others for this kind of endeavor. They include subjects that have these properties:

1) They are subjects that people don't know much about already, or things they don't *think* they know a lot about. For example, if you know all about mowing a lawn perfectly because you've done it all your life, you probably can't do a magazine about mowing a lawn. It isn't that complicated, and most people figure they know how to do it well (even if they actually do a bad job).

But, imagine that you owned a gardening and irrigation service for a few years, and you installed lawns, planted trees, put in sprinkler systems, nurtured new lawns to health, set up rock gardens and xeriscapes, eliminated lawn funguses, and kept grass alive through drought and snowy winters. Now you have something that is broad and valuable to people—something most people don't know very well. As the recent buyer of a new home, a guy who haltingly put in his own yard, *I* could have used a little magazine that guided me through all the steps that I did and did again, because I did them wrong the first time.

Think about it awhile. You know something, or you know someone with expertise ...

2) The subject should be involved with something the reader *needs* to do, but not something they will need to do *again* very soon. Weddings, decorating houses, having babies, installing lawns, choosing colleges, starting businesses—these all fit this requirement.

3) The subjects that work best are those that involve people making a definite purchase in the not-too-distant future. The lawn thing again: Like most new-home buyers, I was required to put in a lawn, or at least to cover up the dirt in some halfway decent fashion (which is about all I managed to do). Hey, I'm a writer, not a gardener!

If the subject matter is something that will involve definite purchases, advertisers will be much more likely to buy into your targeted publication. They know their specialties within your subject, and they know people will need them. (Not want them, but *need* them.) If you were once in the business of landscaping, the very people who were your competitors will now become your customers, your advertisers. Your suppliers will also need ads: the folks who supplied your ABS and PVC, sprinkler timers, topsoil, lawn seed or sod, trees, and so on and so forth. Are you getting it?

4) The subject must have an adequate local market. For a home-buyer's magazine, maybe entitled "Your New Home," or "Finishing Your New Home," you'd want an area that's expanding. It might not be the neighborhood where you live, but most localities have an area that is growing. You might concentrate your distribution in that area, where new homes are being built, but also remember the areas of your city and county that are more settled. Maybe another part of your city or county was growing five years ago, but it has reached its ideal population. Thing is, there are still businesses located there, within that area, that need their products and services exposed to your readers out where the expansion is happening. In short, they might be ten miles away, but they might offer a sprinkler planning service that makes the ten-mile drive well worth it.

Here's my story: When I put in my sprinkler system, I knew *absolutely* nothing about it, and I dreaded learning. I located a downtown plumbing supply company about twenty miles from my new home who would, from my drawing of my projected lawn area, plan a perfect automatic sprinkler system, get all the parts together for me in marked boxes, and load them into my car. You can bet I ignored the places that were closer and drove through the traffic to take advantage of their offer. That was why they offered it: Because they needed people like me to travel to use their expertise. I was more than happy to pay them $645 for some planning drawings and all the parts. (They would have cost maybe $100 less at the big orange hardware store, but the part-timers there would have been no help at all!) The people at ABC Plumbing (in Colorado Springs, in case you're located there) probably saved me over twice that amount by helping me avoid lost time, incorrect parts bought and ruined, a lawn that died early, and about four bottles of Extra Strength Excedrin.

Don't Know Much About ... ?

But, what if you know of nothing you can publish on? Or, what if you're not a writer at heart? (If that's the case, you probably aren't reading this, but let's cover it anyway.)

Okay, you "know nothing and can't write." But, maybe you have a knack for selling things to people? Maybe you're a car salesman who's tired of it? Maybe you want to sell something else for awhile?

Since these magazines require sales, you're just the person to do it. All you need to do is find a subject, and find an expert willing to talk about what he or she does, or used to do. Then, find yourself a writer. Then, go to FedEx/Kinko's and see if any of the graphic artists there would like to do some extra work on their own time to publish a new magazine. (Tell 'em it can help them escape from FedEx/Kinko's and start their own biz.)

You can go out and find an out-of-work obstetrics nurse to tell you all about babies—getting ready for them, bringing them into the world, getting the house ready for them, feeding them, clothing them, keeping them clean, etc.

Or, you can find a gardener who knows all about that stuff, and get him or her talking. People spend a lot of money on their lawns and landscaping.

Find a lady who operates a bridal salon and get her to work with you on a wedding publication and teach you about the wonderful world of weddings.

Any subject that anyone comes up with will require sales. If you're a salesperson, you are already part of the way there.

Or, maybe you're a graphic artist. You have a languishing business, and you want to pep it up some. Find a salesperson *and* an expert in something, put them together with a writer, and get a magazine published!

Or, maybe you are a writer, published or not. That was me. I was a writer, doing some freelancing to photography trade publications, but looking for something more permanent. I knew something about weddings. I sold my early IBM-compatible Radio Shack pre-Windows computer and bought a Macintosh Plus. On that little computer, I learned layout and design, applied my writing skills to what I knew about weddings, and here I am—a successful publisher of wedding magazines, telling you how you can become a successful publisher of some kind of magazines!

Opportunity still abounds in America, *especially for writers!* Take advantage of it!

The little platinum Macintosh Plus, circa 1985, on which I created our first magazine edition, came with a revolutionary thingy they called a "mouse," had a miraculous one megabyte of RAM, ran at 8 megaHertz, and sported a cool nine-inch "black-or-white" screen.

Here it sits in my house, though I'm now using a more advance Mac.

I love that little computer. It works, but it's basically useless. Still, I never want to get rid of it!

Chapter 3
HOW TO TEST ITS PROFIT POTENTIAL

Chances are, the info in your brain earn you some money. But, how can you find out if it's marketable? Thought there are plenty of great subjects for local coverage, not all of them have commercial value— like the one illustrated here.

The following short list of subjects comes instantly to mind: Weddings, landscaping services, buying a new home, moving into a new city, automobile repair, baby preparation and care. Do you notice that they all have something in common?

As I mentioned in the last chapter, they all have the required attributes. The main thing they share is that they are supported by a broad customer base, and they all have a broad and varied group of retail product and service businesses connected with them in the local area. People who are involved with these subjects will be spending money *locally*.

So, here are the questions you need to ask:

Are there *readers*—local people who need the products and services you'll describe?

Are there *advertisers*—people who provide the products and services locally and need to reach local reader/buyers with their ad message?

Some subjects just don't have enough commercial support; this has got to be one of them!

Is there a *need* for *information* on the subject—short articles connected with each category of products or services? My humble opinion is this: There is almost always a need for expert information on any subject, especially when it is presented the way you will present it, and especially when the readers need to buy the products or use the services within a relatively short time frame.

People will read the articles, and they will see the ads, and they will connect the advertisers with the trustworthy information in the articles—information that is directed toward their interests as consumers.

One way to test it is to do this:

1) Choose your subject, and make a list of every special area of knowledge that touches on it.

2) In the yellow paper phone book, look up every kind of business that has anything to do with every one of those specialties.

3) If you find a decent base of advertisers, then you've got a viable subject. (Don't forget, there will be many small businesses not advertising in the yellow paper phone book: It's too expensive for many!)

Put Yourself In This Situation

You are a pregnant woman, or you have a pregnant wife. Your interest, as it has always been for people expecting a baby, is focused on that child. You want to know the latest info on what you should eat and not eat, how to start the child's health out right while he or she is growing in the womb, after birth, and everything else about babies. Fantastic! This is a subject tailor-made for a magazine carrying local ads. (Even if it's not your first child, you will still be in the "baby frame of mind," because that's how we're built. Yes, even the guys!)

What might the magazine be titled? How about "Babytime!" or "Your Baby" or "Expectant Parents." What might the articles be? Here's a short list, in no particular order:

Eating For Two (Gee, isn't *that* an original title!)
Why Not Have That Drink?
Smoking and the Unborn Child
Exercise Do's and Don'ts
What Should Hubby Do?
The Ten Best—and Worst—Things For Your Baby
Is Your Baby on Drugs?
Myths and Facts About Pregnancy
Is Natural Birth Right For You?
Home Delivery vs. Hospital Birth
Packing the "Hospital Bag"
Equipping Your Car For Baby Travel
Clothing for a Comfortable Pregnancy
What if There's an Emergency Birth?
How Much Weight to Gain?
How Do You Lose Baby Weight?
Baby sitter Qualifications
… and this list could go on and on.

Of course, not everyone has the knowledge to write about these, but a writer can do research at the library and online, and talk to people. Then, again, we can get people who *are* experts to write for us (in return for a slight discount on their ad space rate, or an additional mention or larger ad in the publication).

And, one of the unique things about writing these publications is this: You do not want to give an in-depth expert treatise on every aspect of the subject. Why? Because all you want to do is to create in the reader a nodding acquaintance with the subject, to the point that he or she will not feel foolish when talking to the experts—your advertisers. You just want the readers to know a little bit, but to still need guidance from your sponsoring businesses. The advertisers are the experts. You want to "drive customers to them," to use a currently popular internet marketing term.

Now, suppose you put together "Babytime Magazine." Who will advertise in it?

This is the easiest question of all! Take a look at the articles. They all concern specific subjects, in connection with which you will find businesses and individuals who offer products and services. (A good use for the yellow paper phone book.) Some articles don't concern specifics. For example, "The Ten Best—and Worst—Things For Your Baby," is the kind of article that any advertiser can fit into, because every single reader will read this article: Its title practically guarantees it.

This chapter has illustrated the general process of deciding whether there's a market for a given subject. It costs nothing to test your idea in this way, and it can tell you in just a few minutes whether you are going down the right road, or need to pick a road "more traveled by." (It will make all the difference.)

Get The Idea?

That's great! But, before you can estimate your dollar profits, these tasks must be completed. All are covered fully farther on.

1) You have to decide the specifications of the magazine and get prices from printers.

2) You have to hire and negotiate payment with an independent contractor salesperson, unless you're doing the sales yourself.

3) You have to decide the prices of your ad space, the amount of ad space you'll have in the publication, and how much of it can (and must) be sold.

These might sound complicated, but they are not. Except for number 2, they amount to simple arithmetic, based on numbers you can easily discover.

Chapter 4

CAN THIS CONTRIBUTE TO ANOTHER BUSINESS?

Yes!

Synergy, we all know, is what happens when the parts of something work together to make the whole greater than the sum of its parts. It's also what happens when you publish a magazine that has to do with your "primary" business.

In 1990, when I put together the first edition of *Wedding & Party Magazine,* (then called *Wedding & Party Services*), I thought I was putting together a business that was sort of separate from my wedding photography business. But, an unexpected thing happened: The magazine increased by wedding bookings, instantly, and by a huge margin—close to 300%! (The actual numbers: I averaged 19 to 22 weddings in the two years before the magazine was published, and jumped to 64 to 67 weddings in the two years following its first publication. Not only that, but the lady who sold for me, a florist, also saw *her* wedding bookings increase by over 100%!) My wedding bookings continued to increase.

Furthermore, the magazine, itself, grew from its original 28 pages plus cover, in 1991, to 104 pages plus cover in 2008. Its quality, its low rates, and its effectiveness made it happen.

The synergistic effect, looking back on it, was and is nothing extraordinary. It has to do with a known principle of sales.

Pre-selling Yourself and Your Advertisers

You probably know from your own experience and reactions that when someone comes on strong to you with a "sales pitch," your defenses go up right away. Your inner voice says, "I don't know this person or this company, and I'm not so sure I believe this. Maybe they don't *really* have my best interests at heart! Maybe all they want is to get their greedy hands into my wallet!"

A "straight sell" pitch rarely works. We all know that, or should, if we think it through. Telemarketers, with one of the toughest (and least-liked) occupations around, are swimming upstream because they have to get through your sales resistance before you hang up on them. Some do. But, most don't.

There have been a lot of terms attached to the principle of pre-selling. "Consultive selling" and "relationship selling" are a couple of good ones. But, the principle is the same:

If you can earn the trust of your prospects by showing them that you genuinely care about how your service or product will do what they need and want done, you have an excellent chance to sell to them.

The best way to do this, in print, on the internet, or in a magazine, is to help them discover the information they want, and give it to them, before you ever ask them to buy anything.

That's what created the synergy that increased my wedding business. And, that's what made the magazine so effective. Your experience can be identical.

Was it more effective than a "big" magazine would be? That is, do national and state-wide magazines, with their pages after pages of advertising, have the same effect? I think the little localized magazine is *much* more effective in this respect than the bigger magazines are. They reach people "where they live."

There are several reasons. I've thought about this a lot, and though I can't prove it, here's what I think: When I first published my wedding planning magazine, it was a genuine response to all the stories we heard from "friends of brides" and "brides' married sisters" who had horror stories—real *horror* stories—to tell us when they came to interview us. We heard enough of them, and having worked in the wedding business for awhile, we had seen enough on our own, that we were able to create an entire magazine: It was built around the fact that brides-to-be were *afraid* they would get lousy services, no services, or not the services they had thought they were getting.

We boiled down the whole problem to this one cause: *Brides did not know how to communicate with wedding professionals, and many wedding professionals didn't know how to communicate with brides.*

Why? Because brides knew next to nothing about what they wanted, how to figure out what they wanted, and how to find someone who could do what they wanted, and then explain it!

We saw a bride hire a pancake cook (her friend) from the local breakfast restaurant to create a catered barbecue dinner with all the fixin's for 300 people, and then watched as she realized *during the reception* that the person didn't know how to cater anything, for *any* size group! We heard another bride bemoan the fact that her limo was late, her dinner was late, her cake was the wrong flavor and color, her photographer didn't sell her his biggest wedding package, and her new husband didn't take her where she wanted to go on her honeymoon! (And, in the interest of full disclosure, *I was the photographer!*) Do you think this young lady had a hard time telling people what she wanted? I'd hate to take her out to dinner and wait 'til she made up her mind what to order! There were other stories told us—many, many of them.

Brides would come to our home to interview us with their sister, who had stories to tell, and with their best friend, who had stories to tell. None of them trusted *anybody* in the wedding business. And, little wonder. It probably seemed to them that the wedding people they knew of were all unable to deliver on their promises.

In fact, it was the *Brides* who didn't know how to ask for or insist on whatever it was they wanted done at their weddings.

And, a magical thing happened when our magazine was published: Everyone who advertised in it saw their bookings increase. I know, as a wedding photographer, *I* was happy about it! And the same thing has happened everywhere the magazine is published. That's why it has grown. Yours will, too.

Publishing A Magazine Will Help Your Other Business ...

Maybe you aren't "just" a writer. Maybe you run another business, where you earn some of your money, but you are a writer, too. (This was my situation.)

Or, maybe you're a salesman.

Or, maybe you're a home inspector.

Or, maybe you're a mechanic, or a nurse, or a doctor!

If you have another business, and it could use a shot in the arm, the publishing of one of these magazines could be just the thing. It doesn't have to be a big magazine to work!

The process is explained fully here in this book. I just thought it might be a good idea to mention that I never even thought of becoming a "magazine publisher" until after I did it! I just wanted to help my other business, and pay for the processing bill at my local photo lab, which had gotten away from me and which my regular business couldn't pay for. (And, the $3600 profit from my first magazine edition paid the processing bill and bought a new 27" color TV, a Zenith that still works *perfectly* on this day 20 years later.)

If You Are A Wedding Pro:

As the publisher of wedding planning magazines, I have a lot of contact with wedding pros that keeps me up to date on the trends in the US wedding industry. (I *guess* you can call it an "industry," since the direct services hired for weddings annually add up to over $18 billion, *not* including guest accommodations and meals, travel, gifts, *and* honeymoons!)

I am always open to a new alliance with people in the wedding business who are interested in representing one of my magazines in their own area. The only real prerequisite I have, as a matter of fact, is that the people who represent our magazines must be involved actively in the wedding business in their own location. If you are a coordinator, videographer, photographer, DJ, floral designer ... or any other specialty connected with weddings, and you are interested in taking advantage of the synergy that I see happening with each edition, please call or email me.

For either of these, if you are in the wedding industry and don't feel you want to tackle the production of your own magazine, please contact me.

Email address: weddingandparty@mac.com

You Publish On A Specialized Subject

Now, to ride coattails on my only prerequisite above, let me say that if you are thinking about publishing in *any* field, whether it's home improvement, babies before and after their birth, cars, weddings, or whatever, do this:

When you hire a sales representative, hire someone who is already experienced in that field, in the area where he or she will be selling. It's necessary for the sales rep to be able to talk "shop" with potential advertisers, showing them that this magazine of yours is not like other magazines: It is a consumer magazine directed toward helping its readers become smarter and better consumers. Being smarter consumers, they'll be better customers—easier to work with, easier to please because they will know how to communicate their wishes and needs, and happier with the products or services because they had realistic expectations.

Those realistic expectations and abilities to communicate will be something they get from your magazine, and their word-of-mouth advertising will reflect it.

When I am called by potential advertisers for our magazines, they all say exactly the same kind of thing: "Every bride who interviewed me had your magazine, and wondered why I wasn't in it. I wonder how many I missed?"

I tell them this: I don't know how many they've missed, but we can almost guarantee in writing that they will gain enough business to more than pay for their ad, if they don't overbuy. (I always recommend that they spend only the same amount one new wedding will pay for. They can buy a larger ad the next year if they see greater results.) It's the first step toward a trusting relationship.

Chapter 5
WHERE WILL YOU PUBLISH?

Publish In A Small Market And Make It Big

The publications I'm describing in this book—indeed, the whole approach of them—are specifically designed for *small* markets. That is where they thrive. They publish where the large magazines cannot publish profitably.

One of my early magazines was published in Bend, Oregon, population just over 40,000. Another is published in Albuquerque, New Mexico, population just over 1.5 million.

Those were the extremes. I have had requests from people who wanted to represent the magazines in San Jose, in Atlanta, in Miami, and several other large metropolitan areas. But, I've turned them down. Why? Because, they were too large for the business model I use.

In an area as large as those above, distribution becomes a real problem for a publication this small. Not only that, but the entire financial business plan breaks down if the area to be covered is *too* large.

Consider these facts:

    1) Your ad rates must be affordable for very small businesses

    2) Your quantities published must cover the market

    3) Your magazines are published annually

    4) Your distribution system is the advertisers, themselves

These requirements must work together, and they must *all* be satisfied.

1) Ad rates must be affordable; they pay for everything. Sounds obvious, doesn't it? Ad rates, if not affordable, will not provide the base to pay for everything else, including your own income! (There is no "cover price" for my magazines; they are *free* so that people will pick them up and use them.) The ad rates must be affordable for the small businesses you represent—not only in "real" terms, but also in the minds of the advertisers. They must see the ad cost as an affordable, "good deal," or they will stay with the usual ad outlets such as the yellow paper phone books, the birdcage-lining daily papers, etc.

Even though they might think, and be correct, that these outlets are a waste of most of their money, they'll think: *"That's where I've been advertising, and I'm still in business, so I'll continue."* The logic is flawed, not provable because they probably don't keep tabs on where their calls come from, and possibly based on an aversion to change—but it's their story and they're stickin' to it!

So, with your affordable ad rates, you must pay for all the printing, the sales rep's commission, and your own profit. (Yes, I consider your profit a "cost" to be figured into the structure. Real accountants don't consider profit a "cost," instead viewing it as what's left over after all the costs have been satisfied. But, I'm just a writer ...)

2) The quantities published must cover the market. If your magazine isn't seen often by the advertisers, they won't think you're publishing enough copies to cover their market as you promised. They won't think they are getting their money's worth. They want to see it in use, to offer a copy and hear people say, "Oh, I already got one of those. Thanks." (And the advertiser will assume, possibly correctly, that the shopper is in their store *because* of the magazine.)

In the front of my magazines is my telephone number. Its "distinctive ringing tone" sounds off right here at my elbow, and I answer it by saying, "Hello, this is Bill." (Call me, if you want, and let's talk.) So, anyone who has a copy of the magazine can call the Publisher, just like that.

Sometimes (about a dozen or so times per year, per edition) the caller is a potential advertiser, asking when we publish, how much is an ad, and can they be contacted by the sales rep when the sales season begins? Of course, the answer is "yes," but I keep them on the line for awhile. (Picking advertisers' and other brains in your market area is a good habit.) During our conversation, I ask them why they think their business might do well if it were advertised in our magazine, and the substance of their answer is always—*always*—the same: "Every Bride who comes to see me has your magazine with her, so I'm thinking I'm missing some of them by not being in it."

That's beautiful music to my ears. The melody goes ... *Cha-CHING, cha-CHING.*

Now, if your ad rates don't support a large enough printing to cover your market, you won't get these kinds of calls. The quantity I shoot for in my wedding markets is twice the number of weddings held there the previous year (based on the county clerk's marriage license recordation numbers). This differs in every market: In Bend, it's 6,000; in Albuquerque, it's 15,000. (And the rates in the markets differ proportionately, too.)

3) Your magazines, published annually, must last through the year. In whatever market you select, for whatever subject, your main distribution (of about a third of your entire printing) will take place at publication, which should be done just before the "main shopping rush" for your readers. For weddings, this is at the very beginning of the year. Brides plan their weddings a minimum of six months in advance, and my magazines are there to help them.

If you are publishing on a different subject, say, Family Alpine Skiing in Summit County, Colorado, you'll want to publish when the families are planning the trips, not when they arrive. (And, this is a fictitious subject, because it's too difficult to find all those families planning to come skiing in Colorado from Dallas, Kansas City, Omaha, and Pittsburgh.)

For home buyers and home improvers, you'll want to be on the stands before springtime each year. For babies, spring is a good time, because more babies are born nine months after the winter months in most places.

Regardless of when you start, you must plan on keeping your magazines in front of the public throughout the year during which you'll publish. If your cover date is "Spring, 2010," you'll want your magazines visible and available until Spring, 2011.

4) *Your distribution system is the advertisers.* This is an important fact. If your publication area is too large, you might be unable to provide enough copies to each advertiser for their shoppers, and they will see your distribution system as a failure. In a large area, this is a definite possibility. You don't want to run out of magazines and have to say to your advertisers, "Sorry, we're out of magazines; we'll get you some new ones next year—if you advertise again."

Guess what *they'll* say? "Don't bother to call."

Your sales rep, whose job it is to stay in touch with the advertisers and to keep their magazines stocked, can move extra copies from low-volume distribution points to high-volume locations. One of two things will happen: Either all the magazines will run out, or there will still be plenty of them around when you start your sales season for the next issue.

You want the latter to be the case.

So, Where Will You Publish?

If you are in downtown Chicago, you will want to seek a suburb to publish in. Ditto for New York, Seattle, Houston, Anaheim, Denver …

As was mentioned above, the city of Albuquerque, with 1.5 million population, was about the largest I could consider, and I have a feeling it is too large in a couple of ways: First, it's spread out, making distribution for the rep pretty tough, since he has to go to outlying communities, etc., to replenish magazines. Second, there are just too many people for 15,000 copies to satisfy, if they are distributed adequately throughout the area.

In my opinion, the optimum publishing locale for these magazines is a city or town whose *area* population—of the entire market—is less than 200,000 people. With a potential buying market of that size, a magazine of 10,000 distribution, placed in the businesses of the advertisers, can adequately serve the market for readers such as engaged couples, home buyers and renovators, pregnant families, etc. Any larger than a quarter-million, and distribution becomes too thin, the advertisers notice, and they stop advertising. The only remedy, if this happens, is to raise ad rates so you can print more copies, and that won't fly very high with advertisers who have already soured on the project.

Avoiding the situation is easy if you adhere to Rule #2 (See Chapter 25), which is "Stay Small." If you get too big, you will discover the hard way why our little market exists in the first place: Large magazines can't afford to publish in small markets, and that's why the market is available to "the little people": us!

This entire business model is designed for a small market. Stay small, and you can get "big" by establishing multiple small markets.

Bend, Oregon, another small town, but also a destination resort area.

Visalia, California, a small town between Fresno and Bakersfield. Not at all a destination, but a perfect locale for a specialty magazine.

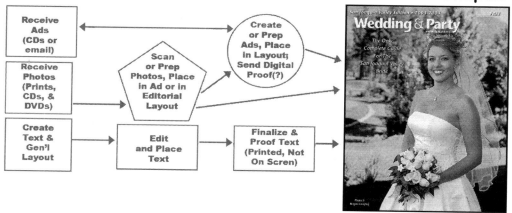

Chapter 6

WHAT IS THE OVERALL PROCESS?

Here's an overview of steps I take to publish a single edition. It's detailed in some ways, but not difficult when taken step-by-step. Much of it is boringly repetitious.

It's All About What It's All About

Much depends on the subject of your publication.

Suppose you're leaning toward a homeowner publication. Hypothetically, your first edition will be a 32-page (plus cover) magazine: "Your New Home." The subject matter will cover not only landscaping, but every other aspect of settling into a new or previously owned house. Some possible article titles:

The First Step: Protecting Your Carpet.

Privacy Please: Covering Those Windows

Colors for Comfort

Hot Subjects: Heating and Cooling

Grass or Gravel? Putting In Yards and Landscaping

Water, Water Everywhere: Sprinkler Systems Compared

Windows: Do You Have A Clear Idea Of How They Work?

Save Your Energy: Fiat Lux!

Heavy Lifting: Putting in A Home Gym

Couch Potatoes Alert: Your Home Theater

Outside Possibilities: Decks, Patios, and All that

Where's the Beef: Barbecuing and Picnicking

Nobody's Home: How About Security?
Going To The Dogs: Handling Pets and Their Needs
Border Patrol: Do You Need a Fence?
Good Neighbor Policy: Making Friends Nearby

Okay, that's a pretty good list. It was fresh in my mind, when I first compiled it, having just moved into my new home a before writing the first edition of this book. (A house paid for through publication of my own regional magazines, by the way. I say that not to brag, but to let you know that this is a substantial business that is well worth the planning, time and research you will put into it.)

Is This A Good Idea For This Area?

With your subject in mind, your next move is to call people who would deal in the products and services you would cover. For instance, call up Colorado Sun Control (an actual business in Colorado Springs that installs tinting film on windows), and ask the owner a question like this:

"Hello, sir (or ma'am). My name is Paul Publisher, and I'm researching the publication of a new magazine here in our city. Can I ask you a quick question about your business? I'm not selling anything at all, yet; just gathering information."

"Sure, ask away."

"The publication we're going to put together concerns people moving into a new or previously owned house in the area. There's a chapter about windows that will discuss differing qualities of windows, single, dual and triple pane installations, and so forth. We'll put in some copy about tinting, to control ultraviolet light, too."

"Okay ..."

"The question I want to ask is this: When we have the article prepared, I'd like to bring it by your business to see if you think it's accurate."

"I might, but—big but—it would depend on how good it is, what it costs, how it's distributed and how many you're printing, and all that."

"Yes, I understand. We *are* covering the market, but rather that get into the details of that right now. I just wanted to know if the publication would be of any interest at all. You have answered that question, and I really appreciate your time. If we get the publication going, can I can I call you then and talk about it?"

"Yeah, sure."

That's it: Say goodbye nicely and hang up. You've gotten the information you wanted from the person: The publication, if it met his conditions, would be of enough interest that the person would let you talk to him about advertising. *That's all you want.*

Call others in the same business and other businesses. Ask the same kinds of questions and find out how people feel about it. You'll get much more information that you expect, so have a note pad handy!

Decide On The Specs

Before you read this, please realize that it's completely arbitrary here. I *do* start my new editions at 32 pages, plus cover, as described here. Yours can be different, but for illustration purposes, let's use those specs.

The publication, you've decided, will be 32 pages, plus cover, and will be printed on 60-pound gloss coated paper, with the cover on 70-pound gloss coated paper. The ads will be "business card" sizes, because it's a standard size that all business owners recognize. The smallest ad will be a "one-card" ad, 2 inches tall and 3.5 inches wide. Other ads will be multiples of this size.

The covers will be in color. Inside the magazine, let's say you'll have 16 pages of color and 16 pages of black-ink only. The printing will be standard 4-color process.

You are going to print 15,000 magazines. (This number is up to you. Let's say that in my city of Colorado Springs, last year, there were 4,500 new homes built. Most of the people who bought them sold their existing homes, creating another 3,500 previously owned homes to be bought. (And so on...)

In addition to those, some homes were sold by an unknown number of people moving away from the city. There is no way to discover exact numbers, so we just have to know that they exist. In fact, other than the 4,500 new home sales, there is no way to know exactly who bought and sold, where they came from, and where they bought, so we have to estimate the total number of our readers.

We've decided on 15,000 magazines printed because we know the 4,500 new homes, plus the homes sold by the buyers of those new homes (another 3,500 or so) resulted in about 8,000 new homeowners in the city. By providing about almost 2 copies for each of the new homes, we are sure to reach home buyers we don't know about, but who we know are "out there." (We'll also reach others who are not even moving, but are doing home improvements.) Based on our informed estimate, we are going to cover the entire market.

Contact Some Printers

Now, you're getting specific! You call up some "web" printers and some "sheet fed" printers.

(Web printers usually print higher quantities of magazines, while sheet fed printers print in lower numbers. Until recently, a web printer wouldn't print fewer than 15,000; now, even the big printers will take orders for 10,000 copies. Our example quantity of 10,000 is still in a gray area between them, so we should call both kinds of printers.)

I won't cover the details of getting the estimate here: It's all covered for you in detail in Chapter 9.

Find A Salesperson

There are plenty of people around who can sell, who are looking for something to sell, and who would enjoy working with you on a commission basis. (My salespeople are independent contractors, not employees, and all work on straight commission: It's the only way to go.)

An important tip: Find someone to sell ad space who is also involved in the industry your subject covers—working actively, if possible. By having such a person do the selling, you will have an "in" with the people he or she talks with. They can talk shop about new homeowners (to stay with the example), swap stories, and become acquainted before the sales pitch is thrown. It works better than someone who is "just a salesperson" and doesn't appreciate the concerns of the business owner in his or her dealings with your intended readers. (I *always* follow my own advice on this issue; I've learned the "hard way.")

After you've found such a person, negotiate a commission structure with him or her. I usually start my sales reps out with 25% of gross deposits. That is, if they sell $100,000 in ad space, they receive $25,000—*if* the $100,000 is actually received. If someone reneges and doesn't pay, the salesperson doesn't get paid on that amount. This helps to keep everyone honest, and it also encourages the salesperson to help collect on the no-pays. (Part of the Independent Contractor contract I offer specifies all of this.)

Create Your Business Format and Organization

(This is not meant to be and is not to be construed as legal advice, but only information for you to be aware of. I am not a lawyer or accountant. The following information is all freely available to the public at www.IRS.gov and in various books.)

What will your business be, a Corporation, Sole Proprietorship, LLC, Partnership? It makes a difference. For example, a "C" Corporation pays tax on its income; *then* the income it pays to you (as its CEO, President, or whatever) is *also* taxed, on your personal tax return. However, if you start out as a "C" Corporation, you can then file a form that reclassifies you as a "Subchapter S Corporation," ("S-Corp"), which allows the income to pass through the corporation without being taxed there: It is only taxed once—when it reaches your personal tax return via a Form K-1.

Obviously, how your business is organized, legally, makes a big difference in your profit potential. Talk with someone who can give you details—a lawyer or accountant.

Aside from the legal form of your business, you'll want a separate phone (or ask your phone company about a "distinctive ring," on your home line). You'll want to get a fax machine or set your computer up to receive faxes. (On the internet, visit **www.efax.com**. This is a company that provides a fax number that actually sends the faxes to your computer as an email attachment. No matter where you are, you get the faxes in your email, automatically. It's fast, efficient, and cheaper than having a fax machine. The only drawback is that you can't send physical faxes out, but you can send text files from your computer.)

You'll want a file cabinet, a desk, phone, fax, and your computer and scanner. Your workspace won't need to be large. My entire enterprise is run from a 10-by-14-foot office. See the photo of one corner on the previous page. I store some supplies in the garage.

Create Your Sales Approach: Roll-play It With Your Rep

Like many others, this business rises or falls on sales. It helps that you will be offering a uniquely targeted publication—something that might not yet exist in your market.

Basically, though, you want to "design" your approach. At this point, you're putting it together but not actually selling yet. This is a time for practicing to make it work. Caution: Skipping this step because it seems unnecessary could torpedo your entire project! What follows is the approach I've worked out that has been successful; your mileage may vary.

1) Call and check with potential advertisers on feasibility of the idea. (You already did this, right?)

2) Visit potential advertisers with the Preview Edition (a bare-bones mockup showing ad positions relative to various articles) of your magazine, some market information, and your rate sheet.

3) Using the Preview Edition (with articles pre-written if possible), show the potential advertisers what you have to offer. If they will take the time, let them hold it and read through it, look at the contents, etc. Describe to them your distribution plan, the need for the publication, and the kind of information it will include that people are looking for.

4) Ask them to choose the spot they'd want if they were going to advertise.

5) Ask if they'll put their name on the ad spot; to retain it, they'll need to put a retainer on it later. If they want a specific spot (and they probably will) mention to them that you can only reserve that spot if they give you a retainer (deposit) for it. My ads all require a 50% deposit to hold a specific spot, and final payment before publication (or a credit card).

6) Keep working with them, but don't browbeat. Try to close a couple of times, then back off and let them know you'll call them again. (And, you will, after you've sold to their competitors. Seeing their competitors' names on ad spots will be a strong incentive for them to be in the magazine, too.)

Do Your Layout and Set Up Your Rates

You have the basic information you need to arrive at your rates, with one exception. You don't yet know *exactly* how much potential ad space you have in your magazine.

If you have worked in the magazine publishing world before, you may be thinking right now, there's no way to know how much ad space we have, because we haven't sold it yet! You're right, if you think "inside the box."

The thing is, my kind of publishing business is "outside the box" from the very start. One of the biggest differences is this: The entire magazine is laid out, with ad space on almost every page, before a single sales call is made. If possible, the articles are written, too, at least in "First Draft" form. Space for photos and illustrations can also be put into the layout.

You might ask, "Isn't that putting the cart before the horse?"

Inside the box, maybe it is. Outside the box, no. What it does is this. It gives you a head start on the layout process. It controls the layout. It limits the ad space and defines it. If the articles are written before sales calls are made (with a preview of the entire magazine in hand), it lets people read what is said about their specialty: They can give their input, signify agreement by buying, or say that you're off your rocker and *this* is what it should say! (Which gives you a chance to change or rewrite it.)

If your ad space is defined, it adds an important pressure on the advertiser to buy the "good" space before his or her competitor buys it. The best spaces don't last.

When your salesperson has sold the ad space you provided, the magazine is full—on or before your deadline—and you go into production and get it printed.

It's a beautiful *pro*active process, compared to the other way, which is a *re*active process. Also, it makes possible the creation of these publications by only two or three people. That's not possible with a magazine that's designed from scratch for every issue.

So, you can set up your entire magazine (with Greeked type if you don't yet have the articles written). You also set up the ad spaces, count them and know how many you have to sell.

Knowing how many spaces you have to sell, you can put a price on them, based on what you need to sell to pay the printer, pay the salesman, pay for supplies and overhead, and pay yourself.

Create Forms: Insertion Orders, Rate Sheets, Etc.

You can do your own forms easily on your own computer; they can be in print and online as PDFs for the sales rep and customers to view and download. (See mine at this link: **http://www.slorates.com**.)

In the Appendix, you'll find samples of our forms you can use as a basis. (In this book, they are undersize; their normal size is 8.5" x 11". If you'd like to download them from the web, go to **www.WriteAMagazine.com**. Please remember that these forms are not legal documents; their efficacy as legal forms is not guaranteed or promised by the author, who is not a lawyer.)

Insertion Order: Basically forms the written agreement, or contract, between you and the advertiser, and can also serve as the invoice for payment.

Rate Sheet: This version is vastly simpler than that of big monthly magazines. All you need to do is take the amount you decide on for each ad space and create various prices for multiples of that size, covers, full pages, and so forth. It's easier than you think.

Ad Specs: Provides technical specifications for your ad sizes, computer file formats you require (usually Adobe PDFs), and so forth.

Have your forms read by others to make sure they are understandable, with "objective meaning" that doesn't depend on who is reading it and what they think it says. You might know what you meant to say, but that might not be what your words actually say to the reader. Because of the way our goofy English language works, and because of the goofy way many people misread it, contractual problems abound. (In the case of the contract, run it by a lawyer if you can, but *don't* use "lawyer language"; it isn't necessary.)

After they are perfected, get the forms printed. The Insertion Orders should be done in triplicate on glued, self-copying forms. One brand of this is called NCR Form Paper, and it is the standard others go by. These are cheap - about 30 cents per set at copy shops.

Have plenty of forms printed—at least two times the number of ad spaces you have available.

Print Your Mock-up, or "Preview Copy"

Your layout finished, with blank ad spaces and greeked (or actual) article texts, can be printed at this point. The details of what it can/should/might look like are covered farther on. It can be bound in a plastic comb binding with a cardstock cover with simulated illustration and cover type. The closer you can get it to a finished, polished look, the better.

Hit The Road With Sales

Now, your salesperson gets to try his or her wings.

First, call all of those people you talked with about the feasibility of the project. Tell them you're ready to begin sales, and you'd like to show them what you have. Remind them that this is a targeted publication with a defined readership that includes their customers, and that it will be distributed not through everyone, but through those who serve these customers. That is, the window-tint company's ad will be in the magazine handed out at the paint store and the floor covering contractor, etc.

Basically, the presentation consists of showing the mock-up to the advertiser, letting the person pick the space where they think their ad will do the best job for them (from available space not yet purchased), fill out the insertion order, and get a retainer check for 50% of the ad price. The sales person leaves behind a rate sheet, a copy of the insertion order, a Spec Sheet, and says goodbye. Follow-up calls can be made, too.

Back At The Office, You've Begun Writing

Slaving away on your computer, in your comfy pajamas, you have begun the writing of the new copy or editing of copy already written. Basically, the writing shouldn't be designed to educate the reader fully; it should only give them a fundamental explanation of the subject matter. The writing should lead the readers straight to the advertisers. Remember: The *advertisers* are your customers, not the readers.

You don't want to fall behind at this point, so don't procrastinate!

If you aren't the one doing the writing, get the writer going. You can't wait for a writer who pushes your deadline. Give them a false deadline, pay them a bonus if they beat the deadline, or something: Just insure that you have the copy you need well ahead of your deadline. (And, if you plan on showing potential advertisers articles that are already completely written, you'll need to move this step up higher in the process.)

Deadline?

And, how do you determine the deadline? First, you decide on your publication date. From that date, you start counting backwards on the calendar. How much time will printing require? How much time will your production require? How much time for sales? For my wedding magazines, which are distributed in January, the deadline is November 15. It takes me one month to finish the production/layout work I've already been working on, and it take about three weeks for printing and shipping to the sales rep, in another State. We start sales in mid-July. I send the Preview Copy and forms to the sales rep at the end of June, and since he is an Independent Contractor (IC), it is up to him when to start, when to work, how to work, etc., etc., etc. (You can't tell an IC when or how to work; that makes him or her an employee, and brings tax withholding into the picture.)

Copyright

The Federal Copyright Law, on which you can find more information by going to **www.copyright.gov**, is nothing to play with. If your words have been taken directly from another source— "lifted," as it were—at the very least, you are guilty of plagiarism. Plagiarism is the first step toward actual, provable copyright infringement. Serious stuff.

Copyright infringement can result in a $250,000 statutory fine and up to five years in jail. In addition to that, if the damaged party can prove the infringer willfully (knowingly) infringed, damages can be added to the statutory penalties. At the lowest end, the damages can be all of your profits paid to the copyright owner, plus stopping distribution of whatever you published that caused the lawsuit. (You give them everything you earned, and then you have to quit business!) At the high end, the damages can be even worse. And, just so you are aware of this: Most copyrighted works have the legal notice on them—"©" or "copyright" with the name of the copyright owner. (Example: This entire book is © 2009 by

William Cory.) However, *even without the notice*, any writing or creative work still carries the copyright: The creator *owns* the exclusive legal right to use, copy, publish or distribute it. You may not use it without permission! (That applies to this book, your drafts of your articles, and anything anybody writes, anywhere, for profit or not.)

So, how do people do research? First of all, realize that facts—the actual information in the writing—cannot be copyrighted; only the *expression* of those facts or information can be copyrighted. This means that you can do research in other people's writing for the facts, or information, but you cannot legally copy and republish the words they use. If you read on the internet or anywhere else this sentence, "The median age of brides in the USA is 29, and the median age of grooms is 31," you can use the facts (if you trust them) of the ages, but if you say it the same way, you are infringing. You could legally say, "Grooms in the USA have a median age of 31, while Brides are two years younger, at 29."

*The above is **not** intended to be a guide to how to plagiarize someone else's writing. It is only an illustration.*

So get online or go wherever you want to do research, like in a library. Read a bunch of the books. Visit a bunch of websites and read them. See videos. Talk to local retailers and service providers. Take notes. Don't copy anything word for word.

Then, set your notes aside for two weeks.

Next, pick up your notes and start writing from *them*. By doing this, you are researching a subject, but you are not copying someone else's *expression* of the facts and information. It is extremely unlikely that you will commit a copyright infringement if you do your research this way. You read, take notes, wait awhile, then write *only from your notes*. Your words will be your own. Remember, the facts and information cannot be copyrighted, and they will come back out of your head as a new expression of that information if you follow this procedure. Just remember: Don't repeat the words or the form of expression. (However, if you write text in paragraphs, and they did the same, that is such a standard form that you'll obviously not be accused of copying it from anyone. The "form" applies more to graphs, charts, graphic illustration, etc.) And, by the way, all illustrations and photographs are copyrighted in the same way text is: When it is created, it is copyrighted.

I'd recommend *not* buying books for research (except this one, of course), because you'll have them lying around and be likely to refer to them for your information. You'll be more likely to use the words and form in those books … oops.

(An aside: The "Fair Use Doctrine" allows copying and republishing of portions of copyrighted material for certain uses, such as reviews, education, etc. If the commercial value of the work is not harmed by the use, it is often considered "fair use." For example, if a writing class in the local high school takes your magazine and makes copies of a few pages of it, they easily fall into the "Fair Use" area. Courts are lenient when education is involved. But, if a wedding association in another city borrows your text, that is probably an infringement. If you borrow their text from their newsletter, that's infringement, too.)

You don't want to mess with the copyright laws. As a publisher, you will want to stop anyone in their tracks who infringes *your* material. If you ever find out anyone is using your text for commercial purposes or personal gain, even if it's possibly "fair use," write them a letter and tell them to stop it. (At the very least, they should have written and asked for permission to use your material.) Send the letter registered, return receipt requested, with signature of the person it's addressed to. If they don't stop it, call your lawyer.

Production: Putting It All Together

Production steps involve these functions, not necessarily in this order:

A) Placing of all text, titles, photo captions and credits, page numbering, etc.

B) Insertion of photos and graphics (photos provided by advertisers). Don't use anything that is not copyright-free, royalty-free, or provided for use by the copyright holder.

C) Creation and placing of ad graphics in the layout. This might be simply scanning a business card, sharpening it a bit in your graphics program, and placing it in your page layout program. Or, it might mean receiving the graphic file through email and placing it in your layout. Or, it might mean creating the ad in your graphics program based on a sketch provided by the advertiser, getting a proof to the advertiser and okayed, and then placing the graphic in your layout.

D) Proofreading with an eagle eye, using a printed copy.

E) Prepping the files for transmission to the printer.

The "Production" step is a repeating one. You'll do the same things over and over, and it will become boring at times, but it isn't difficult work. You can watch the baseball game or the news while you work, and you can daydream a little bit about what you'll do with the extra income this is going to create.

Your time will be your own, in the sense that you can pick the kids up from school when necessary. You can go out for a long lunch when you wish. You can work in your jammies, and, when necessary, you can work early or late. This is the thing I like best about this business: Freedom from the tyranny of a boss and his or her clock. I don't even wear my watch anymore!

Proofreading

The penalty for getting something wrong in an ad, like a phone number, is that you might have to give the money back to the advertiser. But, you don't get to take back your salesperson's commission, because it was probably *your* error. So, you lose 125%. And, to keep the advertiser's goodwill, you might throw in a discount on an ad of the same size in the next edition. More money down the drain. This was another lesson I learned the hard way.

Proofread carefully: It's worth the time spent!

Get It Ready, Get It Printed

When I started my own magazine publishing business, I had to have a deadline six weeks ahead of my printing date, because I had to have everything printed by a computer service bureau on a high-resolution imagesetter, then paste up graphics where I had left blank space for them so it would all be "camera-ready," and provide actual photographic prints for the printer to shoot with a "process camera" and strip into the negatives of the pages ... It was the original process of "layout and paste up." It took a lot of time, and the simplest things were hard, like getting pasted lines of type *perfectly* level.

Now, thanks to computers, almost all of this has been eliminated.

A page layout program and a graphics program, in conjunction with a scanner, can do everything that used to be done on the paste up board—faster, easier, and more accurately. And, it's even easier to learn how to operate them than it was to learn how to do good, clean paste up!

Wonderful technology. There are times we curse it, but for the most part, it's a great benefit. And now that we have high-bandwidth email, life is *really* good.

After your publication is all put together in your page layout program, the simplest thing is to put it all on a CD and send it to the printer as a collection of digital files, along with one copy of the whole thing printed on your own laser printer or inkjet printer. From 1993 to 2005, my sheet fed printer (Sundance Press) was in Tucson, Arizona. I'm in Colorado Springs, Colorado. I never even went to the printing plant! Now, I'm using a web press in Denver (American Web), and I did visit them to see their magnificent twin $11 million presses, one of which runs my measly 10,000 copies of a full color, 104 page magazine—are you ready for this— in *fifteen minutes*! Times indeed have changed.

There's more in Chapter 20, on Production, detailing all you need to know.

Receive the Magazines and Distribute Some

You can have the magazines shipped right to your door, or right to your salesperson's door, if (like me) you have your salesperson do the distribution. It should be made a part of your contract with the salesperson.

The magazines can be distributed at all of the advertisers' locations, plus other locations that fit the subject. (For instance, a stack of "Baby Time" magazine would be fitting at the hospital.)

You should distribute at least a third to half of the magazines the first time around. Depending on where they "move" the fastest, you can replenish them at regular intervals.

Stay In Touch With Advertisers

Customer service is king. In this current competitive business climate, you must be the most friendly, fair and easy to work with, or the customer will go somewhere else!

Stay in touch with the customers. Call them once in awhile to see how things are going, if they have any comments or suggestions for the magazine, or if they'd like to see something new or different. Ask them what customers say, if anything, about the publications. Show them you're interested in their business.

Here's the bottom line: *Your* business, whatever else it is, consists of making *their* business look as good as possible and helping them improve their profit picture by bringing them more calls, more customers and potentially more sales than they had without your magazine. That's it. If their business improves, they will like your magazine, and they will advertise in it again, and again, and again.

Your business will grow only if you help their business to grow: It's a fact of life.

The Overview is Over

On to the details!

Chapter 7

Basically the same, these two editions are published within 100 miles of each other. They serve a unique function that no book could serve—two markets using the same basic information—and provide double the income with very little extra work!

WHY A MAGAZINE, NOT A BOOK?

You can sell a commercially published book one time to each customer and receive a certain amount of money for each sale. If you printed and sold 10,000 books, and made $2.40, or 20%, on each book that sold for $12.00, you would make $24,000. You could publish the book once—maybe more if it sold well.

Or, you can format the same information as a magazine and sell advertising in connection with it, in multiple editions. You can easily earn $10,000 per year or more, each year, on each edition, for as long as you can keep updating and republishing. And, you can do it in more than one location. You don't have to do book tours and signings, either.

The writing you do for a book must be detailed, all-inclusive, and leave the reader well-educated on the subject. In this kind of magazine, on the other hand, you don't want to fully educate the reader: You want your advertisers to have an opportunity to do that. So the writing, being less detailed, is easier. You can publish each year with minimal rewriting, covering only the changes in your subject matter, while still giving the reader current, usable information.

You can publish in any city or location that offers a market for your subject matter. In my case, the subject of weddings exists everywhere people fall in love. That doesn't leave out anyplace! The subjects of babies, new homeowners, dieters, sports enthusiasts, and many others offer almost the same widespread applicability.

You can publish your magazines at the same time in multiple locations in the same state, using almost identical text, but substituting different photos and dropping in different ads. The covers can be different, but the entire layout can be generally the same.

The nice thing is that you'll earn about the same amount of profit on each edition. You'll provide the same useful product and advertising service in each location. (You'll get two or three times the income, with basically the same text and some additional production work.)

So, would you prefer to write a book (if you are a writer) and publish it one time, or would you rather publish similar magazines in multiple locations and earn multiple incomes on them, many years in a row? The prestige of publishing a book is nice, but it won't buy the groceries! If your goal is to fulfill you dreams by writing books, write books. But if your goal is to use your talents to provide yourself a good living, create these magazine-type publications.

"And, *why*," you might ask, "is this guy recommending we don't write a book, and the place he's saying that is in a *book*?"

Easy question. This magazine business model relies on a geographically homogeneous market: Everyone who is an advertiser, along with most of their customers, have to be in the same small market area. I doubt that the present subject would have enough interested people in a small market, as advertisers or as readers. And, who would advertise in it? Writers clubs? Stationery stores? Bookstores? In a way, this book should help you to understand the subject requirements of the small-market, small-magazine concept. (Besides, I'm not really suggesting that you *shouldn't* write a book; every writer should write at least one book and publish it. I'm just comparing them financially, for most writers.)

"And, why is he telling us this? Mightn't we become magazine competitors?"

Hey, go for it! It's a big country. There are *so* many markets, and *so* many subjects, that no matter what your subject or where you publish your magazines, there will still be plenty of places where I can publish mine, and we'll probably never be competitors for any market, even if we're publishing on the same subject!

Chapter 8

ORGANIZE YOUR BUSINESS

This little business is easy to run if it is organized as a systematic operation. (Possibly most businesses would be the same!)

There are differing aspects of organization:

1) Your Company's legal and tax format
2) Your Office Operation
3) Your Sales Operation
4) Your Information Flow
5) Your bookkeeping, billing and payroll operation

It should be pretty obvious that most of these are interdependent, as they are in any business. Your sales feed into your bookkeeping system, which is directly linked to your payroll, which is governed by your legal/tax setup, etc.

Legal and Tax Setup

(Required Disclaimer: I am not an accountant or lawyer. The information here is provided only for informational purposes and is not intended to be construed as professional advice regarding legal or accounting matters.)

First and foremost, your business should be set up legally so it gives you the best tax picture; your net income is affected by this almost more than any other factor.

Sole Proprietorship: As an individual and owner of the business, you can set it up as a Sole Proprietorship. This is the simplest, easiest to start of any business form. Your simply get a license, if necessary, from the local and county officials, declare a start date, and begin working. Your finances for the business are not separated from those of your personal life, except in your books. This might make you personally liable for business problems.

Since it is the easiest, it might be the form you want to start with. You can easily change it later. You figure out your business deductions on a Schedule C, which is part of the personal 1040 tax return. You will also be required to file quarterly tax returns, estimate income and send tax payments on that income.

Corporation: The other end of the spectrum is a corporation. Starting a corporation involves a number of decisions on which I can't advise you; you should talk with a lawyer or accountant about them. (There are also some excellent books on the subject, published by Nolo Press and others.)

You can start a corporation as a "C" corporation, and then file a request to change your tax status to an "S" Corporation, which has a better tax setup for small companies.

LLC: In between the Sole Proprietorship and the Corporation format is the Limited Liability Company, or LLC. It is not a corporation, but it provides some of the liability protection you get with a corporation—hence the name. The LLC can file taxes as an S Corporation, by filing a request for the change with the Internal Revenue Service. (Forms for this purpose are all available on the internet at **http://www.irs.gov**.)

Your payroll situation will be affected by your business format, too. Consider it carefully. Talk to an accountant.

Office Operation

For this business, with all the details involved, it is essential that you set up an efficient information flow.

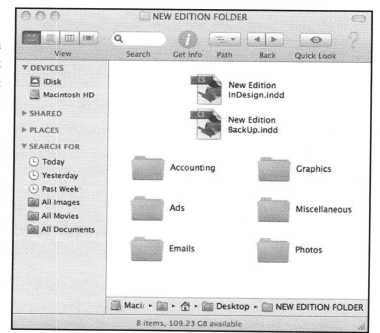

Almost everything will be done on your computer, except the contracts and physical checks. You know best how to organize your computer, of course, but here's what I do: I create a new folder for each edition. Call it **New Edition Folder.**

Inside the "New Edition Folder," I put these files and folders:

New Edition File: The actual page-layout file of the magazine (along with a backup).

Ads Folder: Contains all ads received or created. Sub folders hold work in progress.

Photos: contains all the photos you've scanned or received via email.

Graphics: Maps, non-photo graphics, special title art, etc.

Email: Copies of important emails; most will be kept in the email program.

Miscellaneous: Whatever doesn't fit anywhere else.

Accounting: I keep backups of my Quickbooks data files here.

Also, create a corresponding **physical file** named **New Edition Photos**—for physical prints sent by mail, UPS, etc. This "file" will need to be a drawer or file box, marked with the name of the edition, that contains all the photos for that edition, and only photos for that edition. Each package of photos should be in an envelope labeled with the name of the contributor. People don't take it kindly when the credit on their photo names someone else! So, keep them straight.

In addition to these, create additional folders for anything that pertains to this edition of the magazine. Keep everything for one edition separate from other editions, but organize each edition the same way. It's an easy system to work!

At an office supply store, you can buy carry-around file boxes for letter-size files. They have a handle for carrying, and plenty of capacity for the physical files you'll create.

In this file box, the most efficient and fail-safe way I've found to organize physical paper, ads, etc., is by page number. I create a file section for pages 1-3, 4-7, 8-11, 12-15, 16-19, etc., up to the end of the publication. Four-page sections seem to work best, allowing me to file everything quickly and find it easily when I need it.

You'll want your physical working space organized in an ergonomic way. You'll sometimes be working at your computer for hours on end; make it as comfortable as you can. Put your scanner where you can reach it easily from the chair. The same goes for your printer, telephone, notepads, etc.

Set up your telephone to ring as a "distinctive ring," if possible; it only costs a little bit and works well to alert you to business calls versus personal calls. Only by doing these things can you work at home, but still "leave work" in the evenings to nurture your real human life. (You know, the life you work to support and enjoy.)

As mentioned before, I have a TV in my office. Not only do I use it as a video monitor when I'm editing my amateur video, but when something is happening that is too fascinating to ignore, I can watch it while I work. (It's also relaxing for your eyes if you refocus them away from the computer and keyboard once in awhile.)

Finally, when you're working, get up out of your chair for five or ten minutes each hour and walk outside or pet the dog or cat. Take a lunch break. (I lift weights and run on my treadmill in the mid-morning.) These will help keep you mentally sharp, emotionally healthy, stress-free and happy about your work. All of these come out in the work you do and in your relations with people. Besides, why work at home, where you *can* move around or relax, if you don't ever do it?

Sales Operation

Sales, in this business, is the selling of advertising *space*. It is an intangible, and thus does not normally require sales tax. Just to be sure, since public officials are so tax-happy, find out from your county clerk or other authority whether your sales of ad space is liable for sales tax if it's in a magazine that will be distributed free. (You will be charged sales tax by your printer, whether you have a "resale number" or not, because you are the final user. Since the magazine is distributed free, you are the final payer of the highest value, and you are required to pay sales tax. Even on my California magazine, though I print it in Colorado, I must pay sales tax because my printer has a plant in California. The tax laws obviously reach into your pocket from far, far away; don't ignore them.)

But, back to "Sales!" Basically, your sales person will take out to the field a "mock-up" or "Preview Edition" of the publication. It will contain the ad spaces in place, text (drafts of the real text, or "greeked"), and spaces or examples of photos and graphics.

Your salesperson will show the potential advertiser this Preview, talk about the distribution, the prices, the benefits of being in the publication, and the procedure. The advertiser picks the spot in the magazine he or she would want "if" he were going to buy an ad.

Out comes the Insertion Order. It is filled out, and the salesperson states that the ad spot can't be held without a retainer. If no retainer is paid, the spot is available for others to buy; nothing is written into the spot. However, if the advertiser pays the retainer (at least 50% of the ad price), the business name is written boldly into the spot, with the words "Retainer Paid." This helps with sales to the competitors. (It will give just one more small reason for them to buy.)

The Insertion Order is filled out and signed, copies distributed, and the rate sheet and layout guide are left with the advertiser. The retainer check is attached to the insertion order (paper clip only), and the sale is done.

The Insertion Order is mailed or delivered to you at the office. (I try to get them weekly or more often from my sales reps.)

You enter the information into your bookkeeping program from the Insertion Order, which will give you the amount received, the amount owing, and all of the pertinent details on the advertiser.

In your own copy of the preview edition (in a loose leaf notebook) of the publication, you can enter this information: Advertiser name, phone number, and how the ad graphics will be received. Create your own shorthand for this: It will work best if it covers various options: Publisher does art, Outside Artist Does Art, or Advertiser Does Art, and Delivery of it will be either Physical or Digital (email). I simply write all of this into a printed, loose-leaf-bound copy of the same mockup the salesman uses; it provides a single, easy, portable progress gauge and reference. (The insertion order (ad contracts) are also kept, by page number, in that same loose-leaf notebook.)

Information Flow

It's important to create an efficient workflow, since you'll probably be running your own office and taking care of most of the paperwork. Call it paper shuffling, workflow, information processing, etc. It's all the same: It should keep the paper you receive and generate in easy-to-find, impossible-to-lose places in the office.

The old saying, "A place for everything, and everything in its place," applies perfectly.

As mentioned above, you will want physical files organized by edition, with slots and sections for everything: Contracts, checks, copies of checks, credit card slips and records (if you establish a credit card account, which is a good idea), photos, ads, etc. (About those copies of checks: Making copies saved me $300 once. The advertiser had written a check for $200 when she owed $500, and had entered $500 in her check register. I showed up to collect the $300. She denied the debt, insistently showing me her check register ($500). I showed her my check *copy* ($200). Check *mate*! I collected $300 without going to court to do it. I usually bunch the checks about 3 to 5 on a copy sheet.)

You'll receive packages from your sales rep with many pieces of paper inside, and every one of them is important.

Some are photographs, they get labeled by contributor and go in the photo drawer for that edition.

Some are Insertion Order forms with checks: They get "sent" to the bookkeeping "department," (a specific inbox, shelf, drawer or file folder) from where they are processed. The checks, after copying, are separated and taken to the bank. The insertion order forms, I've found, work best when they are kept in a three-hole loose-leaf notebook holding the mockup pages, filed by page position. (You might prefer to file them alphabetically; I'd advise trying both and deciding which works best. Personally, I don't like the alpha filing in this case, because every ad must be referenced to its page position.) By using a loose-leaf, your copy of the preview edition can be kept up to date very easily.

Some of the papers might be ad graphics or just business cards to be scanned and placed as ads. They should be marked with the advertiser and page position, and placed in the proper slot in the page-by-page ad file box.

Some information comes on CD's. In my case, doing wedding magazines, this is especially true. Photographers send literally thousands of photos for consideration since I exclusively use local photos by advertising photographers. I load all the data (photos) into my computer and file the CD in a drawer.

If you set the information flow up so that you handle everything just once, decide its disposition and take care of it, you'll find your office is much neater, you have more time to do everything, and you rarely lose anything. Even when you don't remember receiving something, you'll find you have put it where it belongs *if you have made it a habit*. This has happened to me often. I forget, but the process saves me.

Bookkeeping

This business can't be run out of a checkbook. You will have people making partial payments and owing balances, sales reps who are due commissions on money received up to a certain date, and your own payroll to keep track of.

There are a number of computer programs available that make bookkeeping child's play: All you need to do is enter everything, and the software generates reports, statements, invoices, lists, mailing labels, etc., making it easy to find and use the data.

Again, the *process* will save you when your memory fails. Make accounting entries a habit. Don't procrastinate.

Billing

I don't do any billing, normally, since full payment is due before publication. However, I will issue an invoice in certain cases, such as when the advertiser is a large company, buying a large ad, and their policy is not to pay until they see a tear sheet of the published ad. So, you do it their way. They usually pay, but it sometimes takes awhile since they are big companies. I also bill advertisers who pay the final payments late.

If an advertiser says a bill is needed, it's usually no trouble to generate one with the bookkeeping program and mail or fax it, or attach it to an email as a PDF.

Organization Will Reduce Stress

This business offers the opportunity for you to go nuts if you don't stay on top of it.

Organization is an extremely important issue. There are no safety nets. If you lose something, you are the only one to blame. The best way to avoid it is to always do things the same way, like you always put on your left sock every morning or put your fork on the left and knife and spoon on the right. If you always do it the same way, you'll always know what you did.

When you do something that differs from your usual procedure, you should make a note: Those notes can save you money later on. This happened to me recently. A sales rep's secretary called, saying the rep had an appointment with an advertiser whose ad I had messed up. She had advertised two years back, and last year, and she wanted a new photo in the most recent ad. It didn't get into the ad. Now, she wanted her money back because she said we didn't print the right photo in her ad. I looked at the ads, and she was right: The photo hadn't been changed. However, when I looked at her Insertion Order, I saw my dated note: Just below the "Artwork Deadline" box, I had written in the "Notes" box, "No new art received as of 3-28-08." In other words, I had no choice but to use the old ad and photo, or leave her ad out of the magazine.

I used the old ad. She backed down when she realized she'd forgotten to send the photo, and I was paid for the ad. (She might not advertise in the future, since this happened, but at least I don't have to give her a freebie just because I couldn't prove what happened.) When you can't prove you did it right, it's assumed that you did it wrong: "The customer is always right!" However, when the customer is trying to take advantage of you, you are allowed to be right.

Chapter 9

PRINTING: THE FIRST COST TO CONSIDER

Types of Commercial Printers

There are various printing processes you'll use for different needs.

Some definitions:

Offset Printing: This is the kind of printing that is used for all large commercial jobs, like books, newspapers, magazines, etc. It is completely different from what is done in a FedEx Kinkos' copy shop.

Web Offset Printing: It's called a "web" printer because that's what they call the huge roll of paper that starts out at one end of the printing press and unrolls to feed all the way through. The "web" looks like a ten-foot-tall, two-ton roll of bathroom tissue without perforations. It's just a really big roll of paper.

The paper is fed through the printing press where it goes between sets of rollers that print the image onto both sides of the paper (at the same time) and then it gets folded, bound and trimmed. In old movies, whenever there was a major headline, we were usually shown a short clip of paper running through a web press and getting folded, wrapped and then tossed onto the sidewalk where the paper sellers would start yelling "Extra, Extra!"

Web printers can print on thinner paper than sheet fed printers, and they are less expensive per unit for larger print runs, but the economy doesn't kick in until you get into larger quantities, usually with a minimum of about 10,000 or 15,000.

I use a web printer in Denver, American Web, whose two $11 *million* dollar presses can run 10,000 of my full-color 104-page magazine in 15 minutes. Amazing.

Sheet fed Offset Printers: These printers are used for shorter print runs. The printer I started out using specializes in "short runs," of under ten thousand copies. The quality found in sheet fed printing in the past was often higher than that in web plants, but that has changed in later years as the technology of web printing has improved. Now, it's practically impossible to tell the difference. The reason I used sheet fed printing for my early magazines was because the cost of using a web printer for quantities of ten thousand and under was once higher.

Sheet fed printing offers the use of heavier papers than web printing. This is mainly out of necessity, because when the paper is run sheet by sheet, thicker is better. Thin paper can wrinkle in the press, stopping production, slowing things down, etc.

Photocopying: FedEx Kinko's and other local copy shops use the process of "xerography" to make photocopies, even if they don't use "Xerox" brand copiers to do it. Like the word "Kleenex," though, the word "Xerox" has become a generic term used to designate a photocopy or the process of photocopying. However, that's an incorrect use of the word "Xerox" (and actually illegal, if used in print).

You will use photocopying for the creation of some of your forms, such as rate sheets, layout guides, etc.

Small Printers: There's one other kind of commercial printer, actually a "sheet fed" variety, but it is the kind of little business that specializes in forms and booklets that can be printed on paper no larger than 11" x 17". They have almost all disappeared, and their little presses are now seen in museums, along with rotary dial phones and mimeograph machines.

Getting Estimates on the Magazines

You'll need to know the following to tell the printers. You have to tell them all exactly the same "specs" or "specifications" so you can compare their prices. If you intend to choose a printer based on price, you can do it based on just one round of estimates, because the lowest on one job will probably be the lowest on any job.

I will provide a set of specs here that I use for my basic preview editions. Once in awhile, pages are added or subtracted, but because of the way we do our sales, the final product is pretty close to what we specify.

Trim size: (final bound size): 8.5 inches wide, 11.0 inches tall.

Quantity: 10,200 (10,000 shipped to rep, balance to publisher)

Shipping: Truck, best way. Boxed with boxes weighing under 40 pounds. *[This will give you about 80 to 140 magazines per box, and it is only specified this way so that the boxes won't be too heavy to handle. With 10,000 magazines, there will be about 80 to 100 boxes. Moving them around can be hard on your rep's back.]*

How transmitted to Printer: Digital files as Adobe PDFs.

Proofs Required: BlueLine of entire publication.

Printing date: To Be Determined

Cover: 70 lb Gloss Cover-weight (house gloss), 4/4. *[This means it's 4-color (full-color) on both sides, that the paper is a 70-lb cover stock, slightly heavier than the text paper will be, and that it's on "house gloss" paper. This is less expensive than ordering that a specific glossy paper by a particular manufacturer. And few people care or even know there's a difference.]*

Body: 104 pages, 60 lb Gloss Text-weight (house gloss), all 4/4. *[4/4 means 4-color process printing in CMYK throughout. "CMYK" means Cyan, Magenta, Yellow and Black: These are the four "process" ink colors that comprise all full-color, or four-color, printing on almost all the magazines you've ever looked at.]*

Binding: Saddle Stitch (or Perfect Bound). *[Saddle Stitch is the "Staple through the fold" kind of binding. Two or three staples are driven into the fold. Perfect Bound is the square, glued type of binding. Perfect binding requires a certain number of numbered pages, usually above 72 but this varies between printers.]*

Just that information will get you a completed "pro forma" estimate from any printer; they, and you, know that some of the specifics might change, and they can't give you a hard-and-fast "bid" on the printing until the job is ready to go and you can provide absolutely specific information on it. But, that is really never necessary at this level. If you were printing half a million copies, it would be important. For 10,000 or so, it isn't.

What you'll get back is a one-page document that describes the specific costs for the project you've outlined. (By the way, it isn't necessary to use a local printer. For fourteen years, I used Sundance Press, in Tucson, Arizona, and I never even went to their plant or met anyone there! However, their phone support and their work are top notch, if you are looking for a sheet fed printer for 10,000 or so quantity.)

Form for Figuring Costs

The costs you'll need to figure on from the printer will include basic printing services, plus any special services you might require, such as color proofs (a standard item for covers, but not always standard for other color photos or ads in the magazine).

Feel free to make additional copies of the form on the next pages.

PRINTING COST ESTIMATING FORM

Project Name _____

Current Date _____ Print Date_____

Quantity _____

Body Pages_____ Body Paper Stock _____

Body Pages in 1-color _____ Body Pages in 4-color _____

Cover Colors_____ Cover Paper Stock_____

Binding_____ Trim Size _____

Additional Items:

Blueline Proof (included?) _____

Color Cover Proof _____

Payment Arrangements_____

_____

_____

Shipping to: _____

_____

_____

[THE SECTION BELOW IS FOR YOUR USE ONLY]

Estimated Revenue if 75% of Ads Sold: _____

Estimated Printing Cost (from printer) Based on Above: _____

Estimated Shipping Cost Based on Above: _____

TOTAL PRINTING ESTIMATE: _____

Other Costs:

In-house Production Costs:* _____

Salesman Commission if 75% Sellout: _____

Profit if 75% Sellout: _____

*Production costs are actual expenses for this edition; not counting overhead.

PRINTING COST FORM for my 2009 Edn of Wedding & Party

Project Name _____ Wedding & Party Magazine_____

Current Date _____ Print Date_____ Dec 2008 _____

Quantity _____ 9,000 _____

Body Pages_____ 104 ___ Body Paper Stock _____ 70# Gloss Text_____

Body Pages in 1-color _____ 0 _____ Body Pages in 4-color _ 104 ___

Cover Colors_____ 4-color _____ Cover Paper Stock_____ 80# Cover Gloss

Binding___Perfect_____ Trim Size _____ 8.375" x 10.875"_____

Additional Items:

Blueline Proof (included?) _ Blueline and Color PrePress Proofs _____

Color Cover Proof _____Included _____

Payment Arrangements_____ Prepay: 2% Discount_____

_____

_____

Shipping to: _____ Sales Rep _____

_____

_____

[THE SECTION BELOW IS FOR YOUR USE ONLY]

Estimated Revenue if 75% of Ads Sold: _____ $85,000_____

Estimated Printing Cost (from printer) Based on Above: ___ $23,000_____

Estimated Shipping Cost Based on Above: _____ $ 1,500 _____

TOTAL PRINTING ESTIMATE: $24,500 _____

Other Costs:

In-house Production Costs:* _____ $200 __ Proofing copies, paper, ink ___

Salesman Commission if 75% Sellout: (85,000 *25%) = $21,250 _____

Profit if 75% Sellout: _____ $39,050 _____

*Production costs are actual expenses for this edition; not counting overhead.

Chapter 10

"HIRING" AN INDEPENDENT CONTRACTOR SALESPERSON

Can You Sell?

If you can do your own sales, congratulations. That's fantastic. You'll have a higher profit margin, earn more money from every edition you do, and have fewer people-problems to deal with.

You'll be very busy, pushed to the limit at times, and you'll earn every penny of your profit.

But, don't cut your prices! Just because you *can* lower prices and still earn a given amount, doesn't mean you *should* do so. If you're doing the publishing and the sales, you should be paid for both jobs at the same rate you'd pay yourself plus another person.

If you're like me, though, you are not a salesman and you know it. I'm not a salesman; to me, it is just too difficult. I can sell things to people if they ask me to sell to them, like I used to do in a camera store. But, though I can come up with sales presentations, I can't seem to pull them off successfully to other people.

In other words, I was fine as a wedding photographer, where Brides and Grooms came to see us, we showed them our stuff, and they either signed up or they didn't. We knew that they would either call back and sign up with us, or someone else would call for the same date. We didn't have to "sell." We just "described."

The difference between my personality and a true sales personality was explained to me not long ago by an accountant I had hired: "Some people can make sales, and some people can just take orders."

You know those books that are titled something like, "The Sale Starts With 'No'"? Those are for the sales personality. When someone says "no" to me, I suddenly feel like it's an argument. Anything that follows is uncomfortable for me, and my presentation usually doesn't continue much longer.

I know that I have one sales rep like this: He is, like me, an order-taker, and it seems his customers more often sell their point of view to him than he sells his to them. If they have a reason why they don't want to buy, he just says he'll call them next year. (Actually, this should all be in the past tense, since that edition of the magazine folded last year.)

Another, current, sales rep is a *salesman* , a competitor, gently but relentlessly pushing his point, making appeals, and asking for clarifications. It results in many sales. In 2004, this guy's volume on one magazine rose more than 10% over the 2003 editions, while another salesman's volume on three separate editions in the same time period, with lower ad prices, all either fell or stayed the same.

I'm taking this much space on this particular issue because it's important that you recognize the reality of your situation. It would be nice if we could make our own sales, because there would then be more profit—but the fact is, not all of us are good at sales. I'm not; if you are the same way, you must accept it, settle for less profit, and find yourself a sales representative.

Besides, if you're selling, you aren't writing—this project or anything else. Also, you *can* be the publisher of these magazines and have a "day job." Can't do that if you're also the sales person.

Independent Contractor vs. Statutory Employee

This distinction is one you *must* know about. Businesses have been surprised by the Internal Revenue Service, Social Security Administration, authorities in their own States, and other taxing authorities, when they found out that the people they thought were independent contractors were, in fact, not so: They were employees, and back taxes were owed—by the employer *and* employee!

OOPS!

Without trying to serve the function of a tax advisor, which I'm not, I'll say this: The most fundamental difference between an employee and an independent contractor is that an employer controls the work situation of an employee, but the contracting "employer" does not control the work situation of an independent contractor.

What "control" means in this context is: If the person must come to your location to work, you probably have an employee. Regardless of location, if you tell the person where, when, or how, to work or not work, it's probably an *employee,* and all employment withholding taxes apply. Get the idea? If you don't tell them where, when, or how to work, or how to do the work, then you might have an independent contractor.

Also, independent contractors are available to work for others, at their discretion. If they want to burn the candle at both ends, that's their business. Literally. *It's their business, not your business.* They are paid what they earn under your contract with them, without deduction for any kinds of taxes. If they earn $1000, they get $1000; they are responsible for all of their own taxes, tax filings, etc. (The only requirement of you is that you must send to them a Form 1099-MISC, on which you will record what you pay them as "non-employee compensation." They receive the 1099-MISC from you in January following the calendar tax year, and you send a copy of the Form 1096 (summary of 1099 forms) to the IRS during the month of February.) From that point on, tax payment is all their responsibility.

Don't take this one lightly; it's a heavy penalty plus all back taxes due if you "mistakenly" treat an employee as an independent contractor: If the IRS can't get "its" money from the former employee, they'll come after you for all of it. Repeat: All of it.

You can get **Form SS-8** from **http://www.irs.gov/**. It's a five-page questionnaire available as a PDF, and is the official form used to determine which kind of worker you have. In typical IRS fashion, the form is somewhat intimidating just because it's the IRS asking, and you know why they're asking: They want your money! Don't be intimidated; answer the questions truthfully. Use the form as a *guide* to setting up your employer-worker relationship. Having completed the SS-8, if you are uncertain about what it reveals, you can take it to any IRS field office, where they'll give you a ruling on it. You might have to change your procedures slightly, or go by their verdict if it falls in the "employee" area. Remember who you're dealing with though, and that their goal is to collect taxes at the point of the transaction between the hirer and the hiree. Not that you should hide anything or falsify it; what you should do is design your operation so that it fits into the guidelines.

Below are a few requirements of Independent Contractor status, for information only. Actual determination of worker status may be made only by the Internal Revenue Service, if it becomes an issue.

1) The business may not require the person to work only for the business.

2) The business may not establish a quality-of-work standard, though the business may provide work specifications.

3) The business may not oversee the work being done or instruct the person as to exactly how the work will be performed.

4) The business may not pay the person a salary or hourly rate.

5) The business may not terminate the relationship during the contract period unless the individual violates the terms of the contract or fails to produce a result that meets the specifications of the contract.

6) The business may not provide more than minimal training to the person.

7) The business may not provide tools, but materials may be supplied.

8) The business may not provide benefits such as insurance to the person.

9) The business may not dictate the time during which the work is done, except that a comple-

tion date may be established.

10) The business may not combine its business operations with those of the person as an individual or the person's business operation.

Finding The Right Person

The "right" person for your project should be someone who is experienced with and not afraid of "outside sales," and who is also experienced in the subject your project covers.

For my wedding magazines, I don't hire anyone who isn't already in the wedding business, in one specialty or another. (I did once, because he was a friend who "thought he could do it," and he flopped.)

In one city, it's a florist. In another, it's a DJ. In another, it's a photographer. In another, it's someone who isn't in the wedding business, but who has been representing another wedding magazine for eleven years in that same market, so all the advertisers know him.

If your subject is new homeowners, to reach back to our earlier example, you want someone who is familiar with several aspects of dealing with new homeowners. A real estate agent, for instance, who might want some extra income, would be a good bet. Another might be an interior designer, finish carpenter, ex-construction supervisor, or warranty repairman for a new home builder. It would also help if they have, in the last few years, purchased and moved into a new or "used" home, so they know the things that they might want done and the problems that surface while settling into a new place.

In many cases, you won't find anyone who has done this specific kind of sales before, because this is a different *kind* of sales. So, you have to go by other guidelines. If they can "talk shop" with people who deal with new homeowners, that's a plus. If they keep trying to convince you to hire them for this job, that also might be good (because it partly shows that they might not just be an "order taker," but a "salesperson").

One other thing to remember: When you're considering an independent contractor, you are given a bit more latitude in the matters of hiring decisions partly based on gender, age, etc. Not that you shouldn't consider them: If an older individual is in perfect shape physically, runs in marathons, etc., and you are publishing a magazine about physical fitness, his age doesn't come into play. But, in the same situation, if the applicant is overweight and breathes hard when he walks up a flight of stairs, but is otherwise well-qualified, you can safely turn him down: His couch-potato life-style, revealed by his physical appearance, would not support your point of view in the publication.

Chapter 11

COMPUTER SOFTWARE AND HARDWARE

Basically, in order to create a magazine-type publication on your computer, you are going to need, at a minimum, the following types of programs:

1) Page Layout Program

2) Graphics Program

3) Adobe Acrobat

4) Email (capacity of 10 Mb to receive)

5) Bookkeeping Program

I have in my computer, ready to run , over 25 major layout and graphics programs. In addition to those, I have all the utilities I need, like Stuffit, UnZip, GraphicConverter, etc. I even have "Parallels" in my Mac, and a bunch of Windows programs.

Those were all needed at one time. Now, they're mostly going unused. I would say without exaggeration, that 97% of what I do now is accomplished with the five programs listed above: Page Layout, Graphics, Adobe Acrobat, email, and bookkeeping.

So, before you go overboard thinking you need lots of software, don't worry. You only *really* need the five listed above.

Whether you use QuarkXPress or Adobe InDesign for layout, Adobe Illustrator or Adobe Photoshop for graphics, isn't as important as how well you use them. If you really know how to use your programs, and they'll do what you need done, you're good to go.

Page Layout, Not Word Processor

For this work, you must have a what's known as a Page Layout Program. This is different from a word processing program. While a word processing program, like Microsoft Word, ("*The* most powerful word processor in the world," to paraphrase Harry Callahan, aka "Dirty Harry") will let you insert certain types of graphics, various type fonts, etc., it can't do all the things you need done to create these magazines. Besides that, it is more difficult to use than most page layout programs. (Microsoft programs tend to be that way, as you may know.) Besides *that*, a printer will laugh at you if you say your magazine was created using Word.

Leading page layout programs for magazine work are, in the order of their prevalence in the industry: QuarkXPress (by Quark, Inc.), InDesign (by Adobe). I use InDesign because of its seamless integration with Photoshop and Acrobat.

Graphics

It is essential that you have an advanced graphics program. By "an advanced graphics program," I am actually talking about just one: Adobe Photoshop. It is the standard in the industry, and for good reason. It will do everything you need to do. There are others, such as Illustrator (by Adobe), CorelDraw (by Corel), and they each have some nice features. However, Photoshop has all the features offered by all the others. Over 90% of graphics professionals use it.

If you are using an Adobe page layout program, such as InDesign, you'll find that Photoshop (also being an Adobe program) will be more easily learned, and will work better with your page layout program.

Adobe Acrobat

Do I like Adobe software? Yes, I do. But it's not because I'm just in an Adobe "habit." It's because their programs are well integrated for ease of use and because, in the case of Acrobat, their excellent solution is the only one available! Without Acrobat, it is extremely difficult to function as a graphic artist or publisher in this electronically connected world.

Acrobat creates and manipulates PDF files (Portable File Format). Acrobat was used to create, from a Postscript file that started as an Adobe InDesign file, the page you are reading and all of the other pages in this book. Acrobat took all of the graphics, photos, type fonts and styles, spacing, layout, covers, etc., and created from them a separate data file, smaller than the proprietary InDesign file, but identical to it in appearance, which could be emailed to you as an eBook, or could be sent to any printer to be output as separate pages or as a bound book.

Acrobat works not only with book-length stuff, but also with little ads from business-cards to full-color full pages and covers. In our Ad Graphics Requirements, I state that the preferred format of digital files for all ads, big and small, is the Acrobat PDF.

You may be using Adobe Reader (the free version) to read this as an eBook. With nothing but the same Adobe Reader you're using to read this, you can preview ready-to-print ads you receive from advertisers (since you can specify that they email to them as an attached PDF). Then, you can open them with Adobe Photoshop and convert them to the CMYK color profile you need for you printer. So, with Reader, you can do much of what you must do to publish your magazine. However, you will eventually need and want to purchase the full version of Acrobat so that you can create your own Acrobat PDF pages for the printer. (Hint" Avoid buying "used" on ebay, and avoid Acrobat 6; it was a DOG. And, do not buy a cheap pirated version of the software. Not only is it illegal to do so, but it often carries a virus that you don't want!)

Email

The email program you use is not as important as the maximum size email you can receive, which is determined by your Internet Service Provider (ISP). I use "me.com," an Apple service, which has one of the largest file-receipt capacities around: over 10Mb. Ten megabytes is still sometimes not enough, and you will have to ask graphic artists to send you the graphic files on a CD. (Honestly, though, even with full-page ads, I have had no problem receiving full-size 8.5 x 11.75" CMYK PDFs with my 10mb limit.

Bookkeeping

Just about any bookkeeping program will do. It has to be a full-featured bookkeeping program, though—not a checkbook program like Intuit Quicken. I use Intuit Quickbooks and Quickbooks Credit Card Processing (though Parallels, in Windows XP Pro in my MacBook Pro). It gets the job done and allows me to accept credit cards with easy processing/

What Must These Programs Do?

The programs used in production (not bookkeeping) ...

1) The page layout program must let you to create the entire publication in one file.

2) The graphics program must allow you to receive, process, and save graphic elements to place in the page layout program. For instance, if you receive an Acrobat PDF of an advertisement from a graphic artist, and you're using Photoshop, you can open that PDF in Photoshop, fix it any way you need to, and then save it as a TIF or as an EPS, and place it in any page layout program. If your programs allow you to do that, you can use them.

3) The final output program must be supported by the printer you use. (Not the one in your office, but the one who prints your magazines.) Using the program and process the printer specifies is essential. In my case, I send the complete magazine to my printer by simply uploading all of it as PDFs. American Web requires individual PDF pages, one per page and one per cover. In the past, I sent the magazine to my previous printer, Sundance Press, on a CD as a packaged Adobe Pagemaker or Adobe InDesign file.

If you can send the entire job as an Adobe PDF, consider yourself lucky. The Adobe Acrobat PDF is so accurate and so versatile, and *so easy to use,* you'll be a happy camper when you're on a tight deadline. Some printers accept and print files from QuarkXPress or InDesign. If what you have will work with what your printer has, use it.

4) The programs should support all of your projects. There is absolutely no point in using two separate layout or graphics programs.

5) The program should *not* be Microsoft Word, or any other word processor. That may come as a shock, but Word is *not* used for layout purposes by graphics professionals.

6) You should be using a late version of your program of choice. I started with Aldus Pagemaker 2.0, which eventually became PageMaker 6.5, and then Adobe InDesign. With Photoshop, I started at 2.0 and now use 9.2. I've upgraded almost every time it was offered and I am glad I did.

HARDWARE

Computer

I like the Apple Macintosh. The Mac platform might only have 5% of the worldwide market, but it is the choice of about 90% of graphics pros and graphics service shops. Commercial printers all over the world use it. There's a good, simple reason for that: The Mac is better for layout, graphics and printing of graphics-intensive publications, partly because even in the early days, the Mac and software for it were designed to process Post-script files.

Not to downgrade Windows, if Windows is used within its strengths. Windows and the programs created for it is okay for the printing of some business publications and straight text, but for complicated graphics and photos, it makes life difficult. I heard another graphics guy say, once, "Do you really want to try to do graphics on a computer that was designed for spreadsheets?"

Abraham Lincoln is thought to have used this anecdote: "Once there was a fly who got born in a vinegar bottle. He thought it was the sweetest place in the world, because he had never been anywhere else."

If you are at the point of making a choice whether to buy or use a Mac or Windows to create your magazine publications, even if you are an inveterate Windows user, please do yourself a favor and investigate Mac. As they say, "you'll be glad you did."

Speed and Size Matter

Regardless of which platform you use, you will want *speed:* as much as possible. And, you will want storage capacity: Again, as much as possible.

Scanning

You will probably need a scanner, though I must admit that in the last two years, I have not scanned anything at all for the magazine. Scanning of photos and art graphics was once the norm, but now, they all arrive on CDs and by email. Still, you should have a scanner that will scan up to 600 lines per inch in RGB (Red, Green, Blue) color. You'll be using it to work with your graphics program. (In Adobe Photoshop, most scanners work directly through the menus, and open the scanned image right in Photoshop, as a TIF, an EPS or another format that you can specify. You'll want to open it as EPS or TIF.)

While I used to scan photos and line art, I now sometimes scan contracts for filing.

Scanners will someday go the way of the 1 Mb floppy and the 1200 baud modem.

That day is not far in the future.

Hardware

If you haven't yet invested a lot of money into PC programs and PC hardware, get a Mac.

Chapter 12
FORMS: RATE SHEET, INSERTION ORDER ETC

Forms run the world. We humans like to think we do, but in reality, we're slaves to forms. Alas, this endeavor is no different.

In addition to contracts, you'll also use forms that inform the client:

Rate Card

Ad Graphics/Art Specification Guide

Insertion Order for Advertising

Rate Card

This form will tell your advertisers not only the rates you charge for your ad space, but also the specific ad sizes and other information you care to include.

As you can see from one of my own rate cards (See Appendix 2), I also include some information for sending photos and graphics, shipping address, and a "photos needed" list. It isn't necessary for you to include this additional information, but you'll find that the rates, themselves, don't require very much space. My philosophy is that the extra space might as well be used.

The rates are set by a formula—which you create based on the ad space sizes. (If you've ever purchased advertising or examined a rate card in detail, you have noticed that there is always some reduction for larger ad sizes, multiple ads, etc.)

My procedure is this: I set the size for the smallest ad, then incrementally increase it for larger sizes. Here's how:

Let's say the small ad, the "one business card" ad (horizontal only, 2 x 3.5 inches) costs $325.00, with a $30.00 reduction available if full payment accompanies the Insertion Order.

Your basis then, will be $325.00. The larger ad sizes will be multiples of the one-card ad, but the prices will be reduced slightly for the larger ads ("volume pricing").

Example table of ad sizes and prices, with Formula

	Prices As Simple Multiples	Prices w/ Formula Applied	The Formula Used
one-card ad (2 x 3.5)	$325.00	$325.00	100% of 325
Two-card ad (4 x 3.5)	$650.00	$495.00	75% of (2x325)
3-card ad (6 x 3.5)	$975.00	$745.00	75% of (3x325)
4-card vertical (8 x 3.5)	$1,300.00	$845.00	65% of (4x325)
4-card horiz (7.75 x 4)	$1,300.00	$845.00	65% of (4x325)
Full Page Inside	$975.00	$975.00	100%
Full Page Inside Cover	$1,175.00	$1,175.00	100%
Outside Back Cover	$1,375.00	$1,375.00	100%

These prices are very similar to some of the prices I use for my smaller editions of *Wedding & Party Magazine*. They are each reduced further for the advertiser if full payment is made with the Insertion Order. I offer a reduction from the contract price if they pay in full; this gives them a nice incentive to do so. It also more than covers any credit card interest they might pay, so they will still have a net savings. For me, and for the sales rep, it saves work and time by eliminating billing.

If the advertiser makes a 50% retainer payment with the Insertion Order, and also gives us a postdated check for the other half (or a credit card number, expiration date, signature and authorized amount), they still get the rate reduction. I consider the guarantee of payment the same as actual payment for this discount allowance. Many advertisers take advantage of this, and have often expressed appreciation that we offered the discount option if they guarantee two payments. The second payment is due before publication.

The formula shown in the table isn't any kind of "industry standard," or even a regularly used formulation. It is only a formula I have created to arrive at what I consider fair price points for the various ad sizes. It is based on the number of magazines that will be distributed, the full year during which they will be distributed, and the targeted nature of the distribution. These prices, for this type of advertising, are more than fair and marketable, even in a depressed economy.

Graphics/Art Guide

This form was once an absolute necessity. Now, since everything is done on a computer, and graphic file formats are standardized, not as much information is needed. If you simply specify that the graphic file you need is a TIF or a PDF, in CMYK, at 300 dpi/ppi, you've given them all that's needed. Add the physical size (in inches) of the art, and you're done. Most graphic artists will know exactly what to send if you give them those specs.

I've retained Chapter 18, in which some of the specifics and intricacies of computer art were explained for the first edition of this book. It has been updated, and much of the information in it is useful, but not as essential as it was in 2003 when most of the world was still discovering personal computers and graphics.

Forms For Your Use

At the end of this book is an appendix containing reduced versions of the actual forms I use. They are also included on the Layout & Design CD (available for order) in PDF format. You may use their format if you wish, but I do not suggest that you use exact copies of these forms. They've been good for me, but they might not suit your purpose. They are reproduced and made available for general information and guidance.

I am not a lawyer, and since the use of these forms may have legal ramifications, I do not recommend that you use them without consulting a lawyer about them. Please realize that I accept no liability for any financial or legal problems that might arise if you take and use any of the ideas or copy on the forms.

Chapter 13

CREATE YOUR LAYOUT, PRICE YOUR AD SPACE

How and Why These Magazines
Are Put Together Differently

The reason why these steps are in one chapter has to do with the production flow of these little magazines. In order to fully appreciate its effectiveness, you need to know how most other magazines are produced.

To get an idea, go to the supermarket and find the Masthead (listing of personnel and contributors) near the "Contents" page of any national magazine. At the top is usually the publisher, followed by a number of editors, several contributing editors, the photography staff, the graphic design staff, the butcher, the baker and the candlemaker, followed by the advertising representatives. There are usually about 25 to 40 people involved, even in small, specialized magazines.

Now, go to the front of the store where you'll (usually) find racks with free magazines that show real estate listings, apartment rentals, senior citizens' services, etc. Take a look at the staff that produces them: Even for these small magazines, you'll find from four to ten people listed, including the advertising reps.

Finally, consider our kind of magazine. It has someone to write, someone to design, someone to sell, and a printer. Because of the straightforward way these little publications are set up, they can be done with few people. In fact, in my own case, I do the writing and layout, cover design, and graphics. I've had readers and advertisers compliment the easy-to-read layout and organization of my magazines, although some graphic designers have said, when I asked about the design, "Well, yeah, they're pretty easy to read." (I think that has been referred to as "damning with faint praise." It's okay; I create for the readers, not for designers.)

(Frequently, I've found that the more design staff a magazine has, the more disorganized the publication appears to be. It's an ongoing argument in the magazine publishing business: Should graphics or clarity take precedence? Of course, if the graphics are truly great, clarity and design can both be served. But, too often, graphic artists given freedom will obscure an important message behind beautiful but often pointless decoration. It's a little bit like the situation we've all seen in TV ads, where the ad is fascinating, interesting and captivating, but we can't figure out what is being advertised.)

The reason the other magazines require so much staff—and a minimum 3-month lead time from deadline to publication date—is because their layout is not created until the sales department has finished selling ad space. Their editorial staff and photographers work on the articles, but the overall layout, photo editing, typography and design are done only after the major ad space requirements are known.

In contrast to that, we do the layout and ad placement *before* the advertisers ever see the Preview Edition. It still might take awhile to put the layout together, but because it's done *before* the sales are done, it shortens the time between the art deadline and the upload to the printer. Still, small adjustments can be made at a late date, because we already know pretty well where everything is going. (We also do the writing early, so that advertisers can read what we say about their specialty. Often, they are curious, and wouldn't buy an ad unless the text was complimentary of their general type of service.)

This advance work pays off. It makes everything easier: We can project our revenue in a "best case, worst case" way. We can begin getting our photos and graphics together at the same time the sales are being done. We can write the articles, or have them written, well in advance of the ad sales deadline and print date. And, we can continue to sell ads up to about three weeks before the print date.

But, the biggest benefit is the financial one. By doing the layout before sales, and "selling to the layout," we can determine the amount of ad space we have to sell and price it so that it will meet our desired revenue goal.

Here's an example: Suppose you want a total revenue of $35,000. from one edition, but you want your ad space to be priced at under $400. for a one-business-card ad size.

In order to sell $35,000 worth of ad space, you need to have 100 one-card sized ad spaces, each selling for $350.00. This is very possible. Some pricing strategy will be employed, and some of your advertisers will buy a larger ad than the one-card (for which you'll need to give a size discount). But, it's doable.

Let's say your printing estimate for 10,000 copies of a 36-page magazine came in at $10,000, and your shipping estimate is about $500. That's $10,500 of your $35,000. Your sales rep, if he sells the entire $35,000 in ad space, will earn $8,750, plus the $1,000 bonus you've promised him if he sells out. Total expenses now are $20,250, leaving you $14,750 on this edition in pre-tax gross profit.

Doesn't sound like much? Consider that you can publish several of the publications in different areas each year, and that you only have to write the basic copy once (with minor revisions for different areas). Believe me, once you get the "production line" going, and you master the flow of it all, you will be surprised at how quickly you can publish the magazines. (The 40-pagers requireonly about three weeks.)

Also, if your market and your subject will support the extra exposure, just increase the pages and number of ad spaces.

Don't forget, though, that you are starting a business here, not just trying to make a quick financial killing. You might want to start with lower prices (accepting a lower profit) in order to get the advertisers to see the benefit of your magazines. Then, you can raise prices later. (My business-card ad size ad was $150 in my first 28-page magazine, in 1991; the same magazine is now 104 pages and the 1/8-page ad is over $500.)

But, let's say you need more revenue. You decide to put in 125 one-card ad spaces, and the price is still $350 each. Now, you have revenue of $43,750. Your printing/shipping expense is still the same: $10,500. Your Commission to the salesperson will be $10,937.50 if it's a sellout, plus the $1,000 bonus. Total expenses are now $22,437.50. On $43,750 of revenue, you earn a pre-tax profit of $21,312.50. Publish in 2 locations the same way, and your pre-tax profit is over $40,000.; 3 locations, over $60,000.

Exact figures are used above, and naturally, they will not apply exactly as shown, but they give you a good idea of the potential. It has been proven in my case, so I know it works.

And it's all built on little ads that cost under $350.00 each, and provide every advertiser with year-'round, targeted advertising. It's a good deal for everyone.

So, Begin the Layout

I've found, in the last twelve years, that this is one of the easiest parts of the entire process. Here's why: If you have a 36-page, plus cover, magazine, and you want 100 one-card ads (each 2 inches tall and 3.5 inches wide, or about one-tenth of your page), all you have to do is average just over 3 ads per page.

As you do your layout, you'll see that the average page will have 3 to 4 ads, and I usually try to put from 3 to 5 ads on each page, giving the salesperson more leeway and the advertisers more opportunities to be on the page they want.

Almost every page of my magazines has ads on it. In the last three years, though, I've gone to a format where each section starts on a left page, and has no ads. (See the layouts starting on page 157.) With ads on every page, layouts can still be attractive, and the advertisers and readers benefit from the visibility of ads on every page. The reader doesn't have to search for ads that offer products or services discussed in the articles, and the advertiser doesn't have to hope the reader will search for his ad. They're right there beside the text. Of course, this positioning of ads with text is one of the main incentives for advertisers to put down their money and secure the best ad space available when they see the preview/ mockup copy. It's a sales technique as well as a layout philosophy.

Making It Easy: Master Pages

If you have worked with your Page Layout program much, you've probably run across "Master Pages."

This is a feature of all of page layout programs; they set up various pages that can serve as masters for pages of your publication. They are used for this book, since it was created in Adobe InDesign. Master pages are used to create the repeating elements or repeating layouts on your magazine pages. On your masters, you put page numbers, folios, borders, or whatever you want repeated.

Master pages can have left and right versions easily enough, but that's not all. You can construct a score of differently designed masters for your publication, and use any one of them at any point you desire. That's important, and that's what makes creating these layouts so darned easy. (With the master system I use, I can construct a general magazine layout in about an hour.)

2A	2F	3A	3F
2B	2G	3B	3G
2C	2H	3C	3H
2D	2I	3D	3I
2E	2J	3E	3J

2   (Folio, includes page number, publication name, etc., and may be centered or to left or right)   2   3   (Folio, includes page number, publication name, etc., and may be centered or to left or right)   3

More Layout Help: The Grid System

Having an organized layout helps the reader and the designer. In your case, using a grid—along with Master Pages—makes the basic design of a publication *so* easy!

Ten-Ad Grid: If you are using a "business card" ad size (which I recommend to start with, since it's a size that small business owners can understand), each page would accommodate ten one-card ad spaces, which can be combined to make various ads. The spaces are lettered A through J, as shown below. The same grid is used whether the page is a left or right page; makes references to ads on any page a simple matter of the page number and position, such as "4DE," "5EJ," or "5B."

Using the master page and grid system means only having to do some things once. Page layout programs have a specific key combination that automatically inserts the correct page number. In InDesign, for instance, the keystroke combination that is used on the master page is (on the Macintosh system) *Option+Command+Shift+n*. On the Master Page, when these keys are pressed simultaneously, they print a character that corresponds to the master page designation. When the master page is used for any "real" publication page, the character changes to the actual page number of the page it is on. For example, on this page of this book, which is page 71, the page number "71" appears, but on the master page for this basic page layout, only the letter "A" is shown, which is inserted on the "A-Document Master" with the keystroke above. Same with all the other pages.

You can also use the master page number character to number your ad spaces. Simply

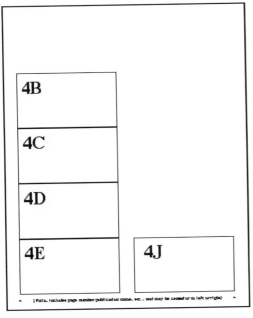
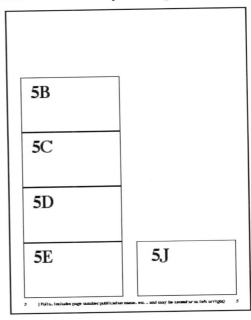

enter the auto-page-number character, followed by the letter for the ad space. To use the two pages below as examples, the "**6H**" and "**7H**" shown below appear on the master pages as "AH" and "AH," but printed in the publication as the correct respective page numbers.

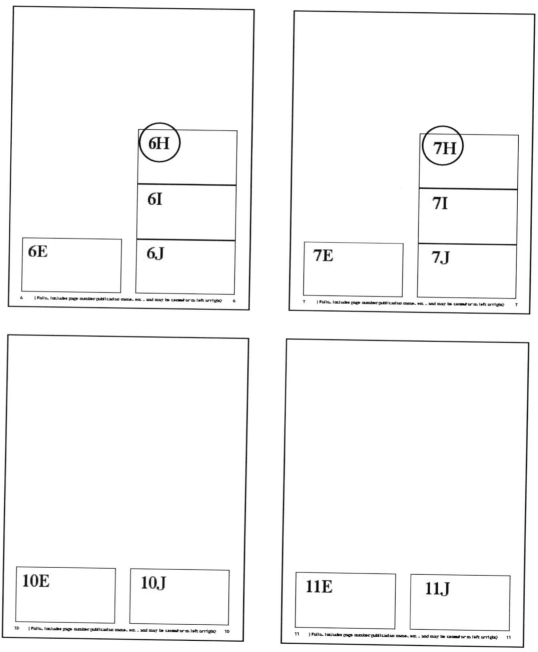

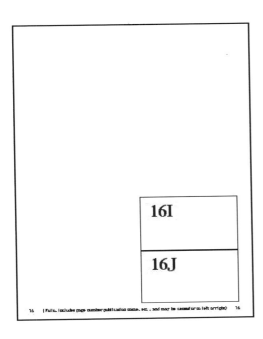 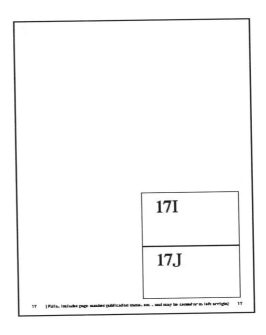

Making A New Master

Starting with the complete grid as shown on page 70, I simply copied that grid onto more sets of pages, then removed selected spaces, leaving those I wanted to use, and then saved the page as a new master.

They were all automatically numbered by using the Master Page Number process explained above. (Their numbers are different from these book pages only because they had to be converted to graphics and inserted on these pages; so they retained the page numbers they had when converted. After a page is converted to a graphic element, its page numbering is no longer automatic.)

Why are the left and right pages identical? In the page layout programs, you can use a left master page or a right master page anywhere you want. For example, if you want to put a Master Page like pages 16 or 77 above on the left, or on the right, you can do so. Or, you can put a page 10 on the left, and a page 7 on the right. It's just a matter of clicking the mouse, once you've set up your original masters. It doesn't matter how many you use, or what order you use them in. In these examples, only the ad positions and folios have been shown. That's all I normally put on Master Pages. Then, it's easy to design within those elements. Also, when the sales rep sells a page configuration different from what you have on the master page, you can easily substitute a different master to match the sold ads.

(Text continues on page 78)

Pages 1-19 of a 32-page Mockup, or Preview Edition

Pages 20-32 of a 32-page Mockup, or Preview Edition

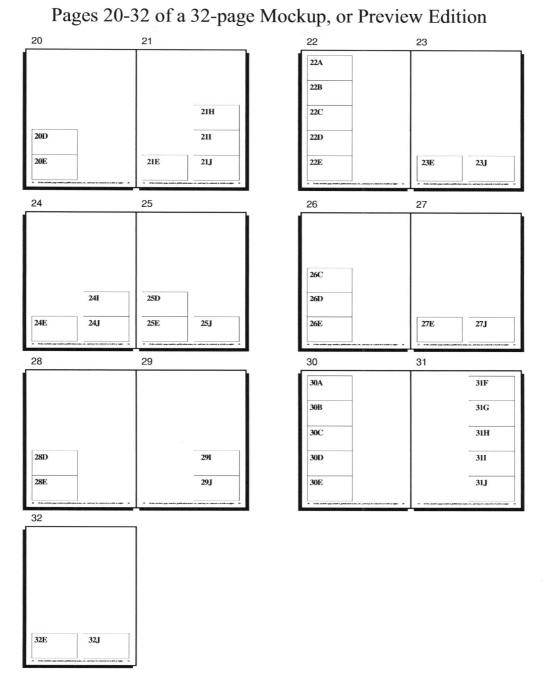

Pages 1-19 of a 32-page Mockup, with text and photo boxes

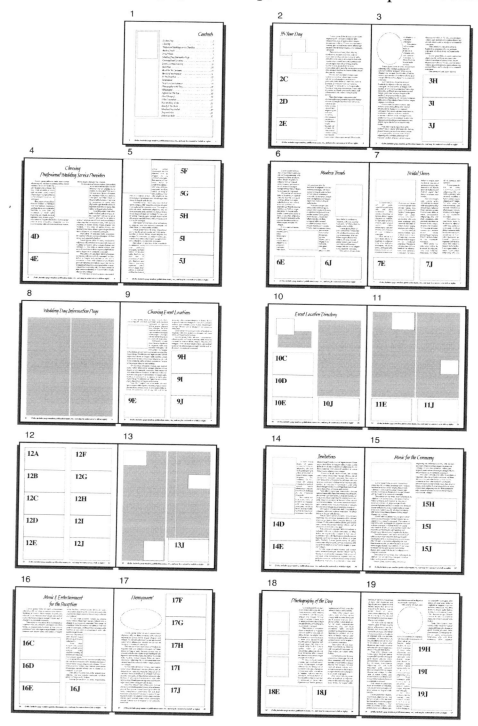

Pages 20-32 of a 32-page Mockup, with text and photo boxes

Setting Up The Complete Preview Edition

On pages 74-75 are representations of a 32-page basic ad layout, much as I would do it for one of my first editions for a small town. Though only the Ad Spaces are shown, it is a quick and easy matter to put in boxes to show possible photos and graphics, Greeked text to show how the page looks with text (in various column styles), and article titles. This first-draft layout has 104 1-card spaces. If you know your magazine is going to be welcomed, make your mockup longer, in multiples of 16, for economy in printing.

Following the Ads-only thumbnails, on pages 76-77, are two more pages of thumbnails, this time with all of the mockup elements added. Construction of the 32-page mockup pages took only two hours. None of this is difficult at all if you do it one step at a time!

Paper or Pixels?

Some people like to work out a basic layout on paper before they go to the computer. I personally prefer to do it all on the computer. For me, it's faster and easier. In a page layout program, I can simply create master pages. It takes less than a day to put together a complete preview edition, including greeked text, titles, contents, ad spaces, and boxes where illustrations will be placed. I then take it to the local copy shop (FedEx Kinko's-type place) and have it printed as a comb-bound "publication" that my salesperson can carry around. I can also provide him with a computerized (PDF) version if he wants it.

Too Easy? Too Fast?

It may seem that I didn't put much time into creating the Mockup/Preview Edition pages. Remember, I have been doing this for twenty years. When I first started, I anguished over the look of the two-page spreads, where photo boxes should go, etc. Then, I realized that these are not important in the minds of the advertisers, and they are the ones who really matter. (They only want their ad close to their subject matter, and that its size and page placement are correct for them. They don't examine other layout elements.)

Also, remember that each page will change drastically before the edition goes to press; the only elements that will not change pages will be the ads themselves, and even they may change *position* slightly, depending on whether a redesign is necessary during the sales process—moving, removing, or adding pages to accommodate sales. (I have gone from 56 pages in a Preview Edition all the way down to 40 pages in the published edition. In another edition, that same year, I had to increase the layout from 80 to 88 pages.)

Real Copy, or Greeked?

When you do your first editions, you might find that your credibility is on the line: Advertisers might question whether what you will say is what they want their ad to support for a whole year of distribution. They might also be cautious because some ripoff artists have come through town, done a sales job on them, and never published the promised magazine.

There is no better way to silence the naysayers (and to get better ideas from all concerned) than to write the copy before the sales effort is begun. It takes a bit longer at the outset, but you'll find that it pays off in the end. The more they see you have committed to the project, the more they will believe you are "for real." Also, if they can read the articles, you have the chance to ask for their input on articles that address their specialties.

More Thumbnails — See Chapter 20

The thumbnails continue in Chapter 20 with examples from completion of one of my editions of Wedding & Party Magazine. A complete PDF of the current edition of the San Luis Obispo magazine is available as a free download at **http://www.WriteAMagazine.com**. It is too large to be included with this book, and it also wouldn't be shown at full size.

(It is also included on the Layout & Design CD; those who order the CD may also order copies of our magazines, so that their quality level may be examined and appreciated. See page 154.)

Chapter 14

HIT THE ROAD AND START SELLING

Business Happens When A Sale Is Made

As an old ad for tires (Goodyear, I think) used to say, this is where "the rubber meets the road."

No business is transacted, in any kind of business, until a sale is made. The salesperson, then, is no less important than the inventor, manufacturer, distributor, or any other major link in the chain that leads to the customer.

With the salesperson rides the entire public reputation of your company.

If you've never heard of a guy named Joe Girard, you should look him up on Google. He's reputed to be the greatest salesman in the world. How did he get that reputation? By selling thousands of new cars! How did he do that? Well, that's the subject of his first book, titled *How to Sell Anything To Anybody*. In it, he tells how he used his own strategies to sell cars to people, always treating them fairly while never forgetting who was his employer. He enjoyed great word of mouth advertising from his customers.

One of the specifics Girard stated stuck with me. It was about how many people each happy or unhappy customer can influence. You know, yourself, that when you've gotten lousy service somewhere, or when you think you've gotten great service, you tell other people about it. We all do. Joe Girard put a number on it: He said that treating a customer badly or not helping them will result in about 250 negative word-of-mouth "ads." He also said the reverse: Treating a customer well, and helping them get what they want, will result in about 250 *positive* word-of-mouth "ads."

As we all know, "word of mouth advertising" is the most effective of all. It is the reason Amway and Mary Kay are huge and successful.

Another book that every businessperson should read is titled: *Influence ... The Psychology of Persuasion,* by Robert B. Cialdini. It's out of print now, but search for it on Alibris.com or Amazon.com. This one has helped me in sales, in human relations, and in everyday life in many ways.

Cialdini felt that there are reasons why we all respond to some requests and sales pitches, and that there are reasons why we don't respond to others. He pretty much proved it to my satisfaction, and he illustrated how and why these things worked. His book wasn't written for salespeople, but for consumers. It was written for people who fall prey to good salespeople—to help them to recognize *why* they are responding to the pitch, and to resist it unless it is *objectively* good for them. Any salesperson who uses the techniques in the book will increase his or her sales.

But, beyond those notes about sales techniques and theories, your salesperson has to go out there and get people to buy your product! What is the best way to do it? Here's what I've found. As I said earlier in this little book, the salespeople who work with me are more successful when they follow this procedure, and less successful when they don't. It's worth trying, then, even if it is modified later on.

You Have Conditional Agreement

In your original canvassing of the market, you called people who provide products and services your publication will cover. In talking to them, you found that many of them said they would be interested in seeing what your magazine was all about. When they said they wanted to see what you had, it was far enough in the future that it wasn't a threat to them. It was also something that they were thinking *might* benefit their business. You got conditional agreement from them to at least look at what you have, and in their minds you sparked a hope that this might be something good for their business.

You piqued their curiosity about the magazine. Now, it's time for your sales representative to satisfy that curiosity. (Yeah, I know: They've forgotten by now. That doesn't matter; they'll remember easily enough.)

Call And Arrange A Meeting

Preview Edition ready to display, your salesperson calls and makes an appointment with the person you contacted before, refreshing their memory as needed.

Preview Edition Is Ready

For your first edition, if possible, the preview should be shown with the articles already written. Customers will want to be assured for themselves that their kinds of products and services are explained accurately and favorably. They will want to read through the article, if they have time. (If they don't, they will still appreciate the opportunity.)

When the customer reads the article, he or she might want to insert some thoughts, have some things removed, or change the way some things are explained. This request must be handled carefully. Your policies should be explained fully so that the advertiser won't want to provide you with a self-serving article or information. The result could be the same as we explain later (Ch. 15) regarding how "club publications" are written—by advertisers. One of the primary reasons our publications aren't written by the advertisers is because the public automatically views this as self-serving and suspects that the text isn't written with *their* best interests in mind.

This can be explained to the advertiser. Here's how: Imagine that he asks for a paragraph to be inserted into your homeowner's magazine, stating that WindoGray is the only decent window film or tint available. However, he's the only one who carries it in the area. Explain to him that this could throw all of the information in the article into doubt in the reader's mind. Suggest an alternative, such as a paragraph in which WindoGray is mentioned, but as a major brand along with EasySun, GentleLight, UVStopper, and other brand names of films and tints for windows. (These are all fictitious names.) In that way, you can compromise with him while still keeping the article objective.

The Puppy Sale

Now, you (the salesperson) are in front of the advertiser, showing off the publication. If you were running a pet store, you would hand the puppy to the customer and let him or her fall in love with it. Do the same with the Preview Edition.

Let the customers thumb through it as if they were actually perusing it at a newsstand. They'll ask questions as they go. As they look through the publication, they'll eventually do one of two things: They'll either go from end to end of it, and leave it closed, or they'll go all the way through and then come back to certain section. This will be where they would want their ad if they were going to buy an ad. Regardless of which they do, this is when the sales pitch really begins.

Start With A Question

You have to find out what they're thinking. Sometimes, they'll tell you without being asked. They might say something like, "It looks great, but ...," or, "I'm not ready to make any decisions ...," or even, "How much are the ads?" If they say anything at all, the ball has started rolling, and your sales presentation is underway.

But some people, especially men, won't say anything. They'll just turn pages and, when they're finished look at you. They're standing ready at the plate, and they're waiting for you to throw the pitch. (This is where the term "sales pitch" came from.)

I don't know what others think, but I've heard that it's best to give them a pitch they'll swing at. Something like, "Do you advertise your business now?" Chances are, the answer is yes. (You want it to be yes.)

They might say, "Just in the Yellow Pages," or "Every Thursday in the Gazette Business Section," or it might be Cable TV, network TV, radio, the Internet, or the local neighborhood paper that's thrown every Friday afternoon.

You don't want to ask if they're happy with their advertising results—not at this point, anyway. (Later, there's a place for this question.)

You want to say something like, "So, you feel that a broad-based approach works best?"

They might answer with, "Yeah, that way everybody can see my ad."

"And you figure the people who are interested in your services (or products) will see the ad and contact you?"

"Yep."

"Do you track where your customers come from?"

"We ask, sometimes. Most of the time, the people forget."

"So you assume they're coming from the ads in (whatever they said above)?"

"Probably."

"But, you're happy with the results you're getting from the money you pay them?" (You want to be sure to use the word "money" when you ask this! When you talk about paying for *your* advertising, you should call it an "investment.") Now, this is a loaded question. Unfortunately, the typical advertiser in America thinks that advertising is a waste of money, or, at best, a business expense that must be paid out. They don't think of it as an investment, which it is (if the medium is chosen well). Like any investment, it might or might not yield a return, depending on the quality of the ad, the quality of the medium, and whether it reaches the target audience.

(Question: Why does McDonald's keep advertising? Isn't it enough that their lines are *always* long? It's because they want them to *stay* long. This is the answer to the person who says, "I have all the business I can handle.")

"Well," the person might say, "Pretty much." They might say, "Yes," or "No," or "Everybody advertises there, so I have to do it, too, to stay visible."

No matter what the answer is, you acknowledge it by saying you understand what they're saying, and then make a statement in the form of a question:

"May I show you how our publication will get your message in front of every potential customer in your geographical market, but not waste money on people who aren't potential customers?" You have a choice after you ask this: Wait for an answer, or pause and then start talking again.

"Sure," the person might say, but he says it with the defensive gates coming up. If you're a salesperson by nature, this is when you start salivating. You know you have a good product, and you know the person can be sold. If you're an order taker, and he says something like "no," you'll fold. If you're a salesperson, and he says something like "no," you'll just say, "It takes only a minute" and then you'll continue. But, be gentle; the person has indicated that he or she doesn't necessarily want to be sold anything. (Nobody ever wants to be sold anything; they want to buy it: *Their* decision.)

Why This Is A Better Ad Outlet

The following paragraphs are not presented as a dialogue, because it takes so much space. But, you want to get the information across in a dialogue, letting the other person be a part of what you're saying to them. Don't just talk *at* the person; talk *with* the person.

Your first hurdle is going to be to show the person that your advertising outlet will reach all of his customers. You'll want to show him how many separate subjects are covered in the magazine, and make the point that the people who are moving into a house (if this is your subject) all need to know about the window tinting service he offers along with the other things home buyers need. The magazine will have information on window coverings, anti-stain carpet treatments, CO detectors, security systems, phones, room-to-room intercoms, chimney sweeps, yard care and sprinkler installation, etc. All of the customers of all of the services are potential customers of all of the other services, including his window films and tints. That is the strength of your publication. People will look through the whole thing, and no matter where they pick up the publication—paint store, carpet store, YMCA lobby, dropped off at or mailed to their new home, or at a Home Show—they will have an opportunity to see every ad in it. And, they will read the articles, which sensitizes them to needs they have that they aren't even aware of.

When an ad shows on TV or is printed in the newspaper, the advertiser is making a bet that some people who need that product or service are attentively reading or watching on the day or at the minute when your ad is displayed. Also, if the ad is in the same place in the paper all the time, you're betting that you'll eventually reach all the people who are interested. But not all of your customers read the paper, or read that section of the paper, or watch that TV show. (And, don't forget one of my Top Ten Inventions Of All Time, which is available to TV viewers: *The Mute Button!* Why do you think they would leave the sound on during *your* commercial? Is it of "Super Bowl" quality?)

In the Yellow Pages, with its alphabetical arrangement and all of your competitors' ads right there, and bigger competitors geographically farther away also represented, your competition becomes a competition of the ads, themselves—not a competition of your businesses. (If you don't believe this, take a look at the Lawyers section of any Yellow Pages. Many full-pagers there! Unless you check the records of the lawyers, you can't go by what those ads claim, because, as lawyers say, "It all depends ...")

In all of those broad-based ad outlets, you might reach most of your market, but you're also paying for all of the market that has *no intention* of using *your* services. Maybe 20% (intentionally too large a percentage) might want to use your services or buy your product; you're still paying for the other 80% to see your ad, at the same rate. And, they'll never turn to your ad. And, they'll hit the mute button when your ad comes on because they aren't interested.

The point is, Mr. Businessman, our publication is different. when people read a specialized magazine on a subject of interest to them, their attention is basically focused on it. Our magazines enhance that focus by putting ads right next to the text—not in the back where people have to search for them. That's why yours will be one of the businesses toward which our articles steer readers. All of the readers will read the articles. They'll see your ad. We've found that they also keep these magazines as references.

Put yourself in their place: Imagine that you've just bought a house (or started a business, or become pregnant, or become engaged, or become unemployed, or arrived in a new city, or taken up a new sport). After dinner one night, you sit down to look through this little magazine, and you find that the articles make sense, they're straightforward, honest, to the point, well illustrated, easy to read, and interesting. Along with the articles are little ads, not intrusive, but right there before your eyes while you read. These little ads tell you of businesses that can help you do things you need done.

As a reader, you will keep this magazine and refer to it, and you'll call the people advertising in it. You will even use some of the suggestions in the articles, because they've been written for *your* benefit—not the benefit of the advertisers.

Begin The Closing

"Now, Mr. Businessman, I have an appointment with two other window tinters who've expressed an interest in advertising on this page. We're only going to have a couple of window tint companies represented, because there isn't space in the window section for more than that. You can see that we need to include window curtains and blinds, valances, shutters, awnings, window washers, and so forth."

"Are you inclined to put your name on your choice of the best of these ad spaces, so you can reach our readers for a whole year?"

This is the first closing question. After you ask it, don't say anything! Whoever talks first loses the negotiation. That's a standard rule in sales and closing techniques. You have to give the person time to collect his thoughts, think it through, formulate an answer. If you have staged your presentation correctly, he will fall on the side of "yes," and you can pull out the Insertion Order and start writing.

He might say "no," and you can then simply ask why.

He might say, "It's too new and untried." You pull out the "Phone Call Record Sheet," a special form you will provide to him that will cue him and his people to ask one simple question of every customer: "Do you mind telling me where you heard of us?" With this sheet, if his people ask the question consistently, and it proves that this ad didn't more than pay for itself in revenue generated, you'll repeat his ad for free next year. (See *Phone Call Record Sheet* in the Appendix.)

"Does the Yellow Pages or TV offer that? No, they don't, because they don't have the confidence we have. They can't have it, because they can't prove the business they generate. We can."

The person has stated a problem and objection, and you've given him a way to overcome it in his own mind, plus a benefit to him even if it turns out his doubts were correct. Who could say no?

Close Again

"Now, Mr. Businessman, we know our publication will pay you more than you will pay us. Would you like to take advantage of this meeting to choose a better space? If not, your competitor might take it."

Again, don't say anything. The person will need to think about it again. Wait as long as you need to. He might reach for his checkbook, or he might say, "No, I'm going to pass this time."

If it sounds like a definite "no," *leave the preview edition open in front of the person, while* you start to pack your stuff and *specifically* mention the name of one of his competitors as your next appointment (which you have set up this way on purpose).

This mention of the competitor by name might spur the person to reconsider as he looks at the preview. The competitor might be someone he *really* wants to beat. You can even reach over and put your finger on the best space available and say, "I think they'll want to take this space. Do you want to give it up to them?"

The person, when faced with this scenario, might continue to reconsider. Your last shot would be, as you point to that space, to say: "I can hold this space for you with a 50% retainer on a credit card or check."

Pause a moment and make eye contact with the person, smile, but give up *for now* if they say no.

Leave With A Positive Attitude If It's "No"

If the final answer, after all of your pitches, is "no," do not in any way express disappointment, sorrow, impatience, anger, or any other negative attitude. The only attitude you should express is sincere appreciation for this person's time and attention, with a firm handshake.

"Mr. Owner (or Ms. Owner), I just want to say thanks for your time and attention. I know it's valuable, and you have to deal with salespeople all the time. I want to leave you my card. If you have a change of mind, please call me and I'll get you the best position I can at that point. Have a great day."

Shake the person's hand, smile, and leave something besides your business card, like the rate sheet. On the top or reverse of the rate sheet, you can put your first name and phone number.

If The Answer Is "Yes"

Pull out your pen and the Insertion Order form and start asking questions about the exact name of the business, address with zip code, phone, fax, email, etc. You'll want to do this quickly, and while you're doing it, be mentioning positive things about the magazine. If the person is busy and wants to take care of something else while you fill out the paperwork, don't stand in the way. Use the advertiser's business card or letterhead to get the name, address and phone number.

Get the retainer check or credit card numbers. The client should get the second copy of the signed and dated form, the publisher should get the original top copy, and the salesperson the third copy. Quickly wrap it up, say thanks and you'll be in touch soon, and leave. They don't want to become your best friend; they just want to get back to business.

Follow Up On The Sale

Next steps:

1. Maybe, you (as Publisher) might want to send a physical thank you card with your card and the salesman's card.

2. The advertiser needs to provide graphic art for the ad, by email or snail mail. Contact him or her by email (easiest for all concerned) in a week or so.

3. If you have an email newsletter, put the advertiser on the list. In each newsletter, you can mention how well the sales effort is going, etc. Since your advertisers are now on board with your project, they might want to see that it's going well. If the don't care, they can always hit the "delete" key.

4. If your advertiser lags in getting his artwork to you, have the sales rep make a phone call. One advertiser who delays the magazine makes everyone nervous. Giving the client a polite request when he or she is late can prevent problems.

Chapter 15

WRITE FOR THE READER

Everyone has his or her own style of writing. Every type of publication also has a characteristic style. The style of writing that seems to be most easily accepted and understood by the general public is a combination of direct, personal writing with a simple, easy-to-read format—written at the seventh grade level. (That's the level of writing in *Reader's Digest*, *Time*, and other popular magazines. And, have you read *Brides Magazine* lately?)

The slant of the message must favor the consumer, not the advertisers: If the message isn't objective, it won't be effective.

But First ... Who Does The Writing?

This is the first question to answer. For my publications, I do all of the writing. I see this as a necessity. When an advertiser wants to provide some information for an article, I talk to him or her, and I make these requirements clear, nicely:

1) I do not put their byline on an article.

2) They have to send me the article with a written copyright release to me to edit it in any way necessary for fitting of the copy, clarity, use of language, word choices, etc.

3) If I use a lot of their information, I will put a little box at the end saying they provided information for the article.

4) I am not obligated to use any of their information.

5) I will not use their article as the sole source of information.

You can do it any way you want in your magazines. If you aren't a writer, you might want to ask advertisers to write for the magazine. Still, if there is any alternative, use it before you ask advertisers to write for you.

The reasons for my hard-line attitude on this will become apparent as you read farther. One of the most important things about the information in these magazines is this: It must be perceived as objective, or it won't be credible. If the text isn't trusted by the readers, the ads won't be, either. It can't be seen as serving the interests of any particular advertiser or a particular way of performing services.

We've all seen association or club publications with the byline of (for example) Sally Sue Smith on a particular article, touting the virtues of buying only from a business that does things a certain way. This article's point of view might carry some credibility if not for the fact that Sally Sue Smith's ad for "Sweet Treats From Sally Sue" occupies half of the same page the article is on. It's obvious that SS was given something for providing the article, and it's obvious to the reader that SS should just make her candy, because she is certainly not a writer. And, maybe the editor was no editor, either!

The reason these publications must be written by a third party (you, or someone else who is not an advertiser) is twofold:

1) It's a customer credibility issue. As explained above, the information in a self-serving article (or one that appears to be self-serving and one-sided) will not be trusted by the consumer. Those who write these kinds of articles and then advertise beside them don't realize it, but their own business credibility is harmed: The consumer gets the idea that the information this person provides will not be objective and consumer oriented, but will be opinion-driven and geared only to "making a sale."

Not that there's anything wrong with making a sale! After all, that's what we're trying to do in the magazines. But, it's sort of seen as unfair competition if Sally Sue has all that space and verbiage, while someone else has just their business card. And that "someone else" might make much better pralines than SS does!

2) The other reason the articles shouldn't be written by an advertiser is simple: If Sally Sue gets that ad and article on one or more pages, Billy Bob Butkus is going to want the same kind of space, for the same kind of cost. Billy Bob won't understand that SS's article might not help her business very much. He will only see that she got "a lot of space with her name all over it." Now, BB will either want to write an article, too, (maybe a rebuttal) or he will want some monetary allowance because his ad won't have the same impact SS's does. On a "visibility" basis, he's right. Also, he might be in the same business Sally is in, and he'll be rightly concerned that people will believe what she says in her article, some parts of which could make them shy away from the way he does business. (Maybe he specializes in fudge, and she says in her article that fudge rots your kids' teeth more than anything else! True or not, when it's in print, people give it credence.) The problem is, his way of doing business (or his fudge) might be the best for the customer, but they sure won't find that out if Sally writes the article!

The solution to this is to write the articles in a general way, not leaning toward or away from any specific line of products, business method, or anything else that might favor one advertiser over another. Let the advertisers be the experts. Tell the readers to see as many service providers or product sellers as they can (preferably your advertisers first), and find out what they all say. "The Advertisers Are The Experts" should be your unwritten slogan. Aim your readers at your advertisers for real expert guidance.

If something is objectively true, you can say so, and the advertisers will support it. For instance, you can state an infant seat correctly installed in an automobile should face forward, and everyone will agree. But if you state that an infant seat with a built-in crumb-catcher is better than one without (because it keeps your car cleaner), you'll get flack from people who say that the crumb catcher can also catch your ballpoint pen cap, or a nickel, and these can choke the little ones. If you mention the crumb catcher at all, you have to give both sides; and you'll lose those who sell the crumb catcher. (Thank goodness, there really isn't an infant car seat with a crumb catcher. Um ... is there?)

What Is The Style, Voice and P.O.V. (Point of View)?

I've written this book in the same style I use for my magazines. It's easy to read, not formal, and more conversational than literary. For example, take a look at the pronouns.

I use "you" a lot, as if I'm talking directly to you, the reader. (Who else would I be talking to?)

I could have used "one," but that's too formal and academic. It would imply that I was not "necessarily" talking about the reader or to the reader, but about or to someone else who the reader might represent. It's archaic.

In this book, I write in the first person. In my magazines, I normally don't. No reader of those magazines knows or cares who I am (because I'm not a famous expert), so the use of "I" would be out of place. If your magazines are written as an individual who is guiding the reader through a process, as this book is written for you, then the use of "I" is appropriate, though not necessary. Using "I" *might* give your reader the feeling: "Okay, this is how *this* person does it, and it seems to work, but it isn't the way it *has* to be done in order to work." (That's also the message I want you —readers of *this* book—to receive.)

On the other hand, not using "I" gives the reader the feeling: "This is the way it's done by everyone."

Or, if you are well-known or your writing is respected and well-known, the use of "I" would work, in your known area of expertise. (Martha Stewart, for example, on making neat little decorated *canapés*—but not in the area of investing.)

The reason I use "I" in this book is simple: I do things the way I am describing, and I have created a well-paying occupation for myself by doing them this way, but who knows what you might be capable of? You might earn *ten times* what I do with this program by doing things differently. So, there's more than one way to publish magazines: I've proved it at one level, and you might go even farther.

Here are two paragraphs to illustrate the style point: One is written the way I am writing in this book; the next is written the way I'd write the same information in one of my magazines.

For This Book: The style of writing you use is entirely your choice. I've found that the casual, personal style that speaks directly to the reader in an immediate, direct way works best. I also enjoy writing in a personal way; it's like having a conversation with my readers.

For A Magazine: The style of writing you use is entirely your choice. The casual, personal style that speaks directly to the reader in an immediate, direct way works well. Also, you might enjoy writing in a personal way; it's like having a conversation with your readers.

As you can see, there's not a ton of difference. Writing without the "I" sometimes requires that you not make flat statements like that I made in the second sentence of paragraph 2, above. Notice that I replaced the word "best" in that sentence with the word "well" in the second paragraph. Unless you're a known, acknowledged expert, your flat statement of qualitative opinions might give the reader the impression you just want to be *thought* of as an expert. (Interestingly, as the publisher of the magazine, you will be perceived this way, anyway! If you're in the business the magazine deals with, that's a *good* thing.)

Easy to Read, or Hard?

Another consideration I take seriously is something called "readability." A man name Rudolph Flesch, years ago, wrote a book named *The Art Of Readable Writing,* which was is about how to write for the average reader's level. I try to write my magazines for a reading level of about the seventh grade. Why? *Readers Digest* and *Time Magazine* write at that level, for one thing, and they are two of the most readable publications around. Also, that's the level at which most of the American public can read easily without having to work at it. I don't want people to have to "work" at understanding my writing!

The readability of this chapter, so far, is about the tenth grade. The average word has

4.28 characters. That's good. But, my paragraph length averages 44 words—somewhat long. My sentence length is long, too. I could, and would, vary the sentence length more if this were one of my magazines. I'd put in short sentences. I'd put in a lot of them. Some would just have one or two words. Really. No kidding.

Short sentences, even one-word "semi-sentences," as I call them, break up the thoughts and lower the reading level.

Word choice is important, too. In the subtitle above, I used the word "hard" on purpose, instead of "difficult." The reading level rises with the number of syllables per word.

Write In Your Style On Purpose

I don't remember where I read the next bit of information, but it's important for you to know and for you to think about for your readers. In the boxes to the right are four quadrants, labeled as you can see.

1. Conscious Competent	2. UnConscious Competent
3. Conscious InCompetent	4. UnConscious InCompetent

The "Conscious Competent" is a person who does something the right way and does it well, and knows why he or she is doing it that way instead of another way. (Doing things a certain way, correctly, on purpose.) By the way, this is where you want to be in most areas of your life.

The "Unconscious Competent" is the person who does something the right way and does it well, but does not know why he or she is doing it that way instead of another way. (Doing things a certain way, correctly, by instinct but not out of knowledge.) Picking out chords and tunes on a piano, "by ear," is a good example.

The "Conscious Incompetent" is a person who is doing something a certain way, with full knowledge that the way he or she is doing it is probably not the right way, but is doing it anyway. (Doing things wrong, and knowing it.) Driving too late through yellow and red lights is a good example of this.

The "Unconscious Incompetent" is a person who is doing something a certain way, with no knowledge of the fact that the way he or she is doing it is probably not the right way. (Doing things wrong, but not knowing it's wrong.) Many of the inexperienced drivers I encounter are in this box!

In your writing, you want to be in Box 1 *all the time*. You want to write in a certain way, of course, because you understand your subject, but also because you know your reader, and you know exactly how your writing will be read and understood (or not). As the communicator, it's up to you (or to a writer you might hire) to get the message to the reader in an interesting manner, at his or her reading level.

Putting It In Perspective

The message should always fit its audience; if it doesn't, its audience won't stay with it. While these little magazines are not vying for the Pullitzer Prize, the rule still applies. The commercial value of your project relies on it.

Writing is a craft. Not everyone can do it well. If you are a competent writer, then you should do it yourself. If you are not a writer, it mght be best for the project if you hired a writer to help you. The writing in your magazine should be as good as, if not better than, the text in the "big" magazines.

Chapter 16

AN ADVERTISING PRIMER

What is the basic purpose of an advertisement in one of these local magazines?

Think about this question for a moment. Try to arrive at your own answer before you read on.

The Purpose of an Ad

There are varying degrees to which ads try to motivate us, but they all attempt to motivate us to contact the advertiser, and they give us a way to do it easily.

The ideal, perfectly performing ad moves the reader or viewer to pick up the phone and call, or get into the car and go to investigate what the ad is pushing. That's the ideal ad. But even the "ideal" ad cannot actually sell the product or service. The ad can only motivate; not sell.

The ideal ad, then, moves the viewer to take an action. If it's an exceptional ad, it also puts the viewer/reader in a frame of mind to buy or to hire—if the reality is as good as the ad promises.

That's all—but that's a heck of a lot. Getting someone off the couch to spend their money isn't easy, even if they are in the market for whatever the ad is advertising.

As a reader, an ad has done its job if you keep it, or remember it and act on it. So, the ads your magazines will carry should all keep this as their primary rule: *Just motivate the reader to contact us!*

Making The Sale Is Not The Ad's Job

It is asking too much of a little ad to expect it to do anything more than motivate contact. It is after that contact that the sales process takes place.

I make a strong point of this because some of our advertisers, mostly small-business owners, say "their ad didn't work" for them because many of the people who responded to it didn't purchase from them or hire them. My response is always similar to what is stated above. The ad "works" if it makes the phone ring or the door swing open; from then on, the responsibility is entirely in the lap of the clerk, owner, or whomever encounters the potential customer. They, not the ad, must do the selling!

This is a good reason why the text or impression an ad gives must match the reality the customer encounters when contact is made. If the ad says, "Friendliest Service in the Valley," and you can't even gain a clerk's attention to ask a question, the ad has lied. (Maybe the business owner gives friendly service, but that enthusiasm hasn't yet infected the staff.) If an ad says, "Huge Selection of Invitations," and the stationery store offers two invitation catalogs, the ad has lied.

The Ad, Itself, Must Be Effective

The responsibility for the effectiveness of any given ad falls on the ad, not on the medium that carries it. A good ad will work in a mediocre publication. A bad ad won't work, even in a great publication.

In my Insertion Order, I have a clause that states that the responsibility for the ad's efficacy is the responsibility of the advertiser. The magazine's duty is fulfilled if it (the magazine) is distributed as promised throughout the market.

In this book, I won't try to tell you how to create "good ads." There are many books and articles on that subject. Just counsel your advertisers with this one sentence. "The ad moves them to contact you. That's all. Then, you make the sale."

Making An Ad Stand Out

Take a look through the Yellow Pages and note those ads that grab your attention, *versus* those ads that *hold* your attention.

Which would you want *your* ad to be?

Personally, I would prefer that my ad *hold* the reader's attention and pique his or her curiosity. The longer they spend with one ad, the more likely it is that the ad will move them to make contact.

You will see ads that are done entirely in *reverse*, that is, they consist of black background with white type. These are the ones that grab your attention. However, they might not hold your attention long because they are hard on the eyes.

The ones that hold your attention are the ones that create a story, pull you in with well-written text (but not too much of it) and that have a good illustration. The illustration is important.

There are many proven techniques for creating ads. I recommend a book named

Ogilvy on Advertising, by David Ogilvy, founder and former senior partner of Ogilvy and Mather, a leading ad firm in New York. This gentleman pretty much defined most of the ad formats still in use, and through his book you'll find out things you didn't know before. For instance:

Did you know that, for marketing to young men, a beautiful young woman is the best illustration? (That's probably not a surprise.)

Did you know that, for marketing to young women, a handsome young man is the best illustration? (That's probably not a surprise, either.)

But, did you know that for marketing to *both men and women*, and to young and old alike, the quickest attention grabber is a cute baby? (That probably *is* a surprise. It was to me!)

Chapter 17

TWO INGREDIENTS OF GREAT ADS

Great ads don't necessarily win awards. They just make the phone ring at the advertiser's place of business.

Great Ads Feature The Unique Selling Proposition

If you started a business of your own, it would do things differently from other businesses, right? In fact, isn't that one reason you would decide to start it? Isn't it true that your idea would be to provide something different from what was already available? Within that difference is the kernel of an effective ad campaign.

Businesses all try to appear to be different. (And some of them really are!) Nobody advertises that their business is "just like all the others." (That is, they don't unless they are a MacDonald's or other franchise whose very success depends on their collective similarity.) Most businesses attempt to set themselves apart in the minds of their potential customers and clients. One will offer a money-back guarantee if you aren't satisfied, another will double the value of your coupons, another promises it will deliver packages overnight without fail, and another sends wonderful high quality frozen-hard steaks packed in dry ice with a reusable cooler as the shipping container.

A *Unique Selling Proposition*, or USP, is what one business offers that is unique. Why is Joe's Yard Care the one you should choose? Is it because they mow lawns nicely? No, they all do that. In fact, so could you. But, for the same price all the others charge just to mow the grass, Joe's Yard Care trims your bushes and adjusts your sprinklers, and once a year, if you need it, Joe's will aerate your yard. All you have to do is sign a one-year contract.

Carly's Lawn Service, on the other hand, just mows the lawn, but Carly does it personally, in a bikini. She looks quite good in that bikini, and she smiles at you while she works. Carly's USP is especially unique; Joe could never compete with it. Single guys hire Carly. Not surprisingly, families hire Joe.

Joe's extra service and Carly's display of flesh are their USPs. Nobody else offers them.

They can each carve out a portion of the market through the use of their USP.

Guarantees of satisfaction ... a refund of the difference if you find a lower price ... overnight delivery or your money back ... money back if your wait is more than 7 minutes ... a babe in a bikini ... these are all USP's. If your advertisers offer one, they should display it prominently in their ads. If they don't, they should discover theirs or create it.

The question they must ask is: Why should a potential customer hire me or buy from me *instead* of my competitors? The answer needs to be compelling. If it is, it can revolutionize a small business'es ad results.

Great Ads Sell Benefits

Product businesses all sell basically the same products. Service businesses, like Joe's and Carly's, above, offer the same basic services. Products and services all have features, and they all have benefits to match them. (Small size is a feature; "take it with you everywhere" is a benefit.) Along with the USP, the ads of a business should sell the benefits rather than features.

What's the real difference? Features of a product are what it is and what it does: They are tangible. A lawnmower mows the lawn. A dishwasher washes the dishes. But, a lawnmower that is self-propelled and easy to turn offers a specific benefit: It's easy to use. Maybe they could say, "It's so easy to use, you won't even break a sweat." The dishwasher folks could claim, "Even hard water won't leave spots."

A feature of Carly's Lawn Service would be that she mows lawns, wears a bikini and looks great in it. A *benefit* Carly could offer might be, "You are welcome to watch."

A feature of Joe's could be that he trims bushes and monitors sprinkler settings; the benefit would be, "You don't have to anything to maintain your lawn."

Benefits are often something you *won't* have to do. Benefits are usually intangible; they are what *you* get out of using a specific product or service, as provided by a specific business, beyond the tangible function performed. They answer the question the customer always asks to himself or herself: "What's In It For Me?"

In service businesses, how do you sell benefits? What's the benefit of hiring a lawn service instead of doing it yourself? "Never own another lawnmower." How about a car wash? "Don't get your feet wet."

How about a foot-washer manufacturer? "Get your feet wet."

Chapter 18

A GRAPHICS PRIMER

This chapter is designed to give the graphics novice some basic, clear information regarding a confusing area. If you are a working graphic artist or if you have experience with graphics for print, this chapter might still be helpful.

The Printer You Will Use

I mentioned earlier that you have two major choices in types of printers: Web and sheet fed. Regarding the graphics used, it doesn't matter which kind of printing press is being used.

What Is A "Graphic?"

A "graphic" is any item included on your page that isn't type.

On this page, for instance, the only added "graphic" is the Tool Menu from my InDesign application, which I grabbed with my screenshot keys. (Notice that the word *graphic* can be used as a singular noun, referring to a single graphic element on a page.) Everything else on the page is "type," which is not considered a graphic.

(Type becomes a design element just by being on the page. However, for this chapter, we're not talking about type and graphics as parts of the design; we're only addressing them as specific kinds of items. Sometimes, a graphic is just a graphic.)

Basically, the term "graphics" refers collectively to illustrative items on your pages and throughout your publication. A graphic can be a straight line, or it can be the Mona Lisa. It can be a photograph, or it can be a drawing created by a 5-year-old.

How Things Are Printed On Paper

Bear with me; you probably know this. But, for the uninformed:

Take a close look with a magnifying glass at anything printed on any piece of paper.

Whether it's in a color, many colors, or black and white, everything you see printed on any piece of paper is printed in the same way.

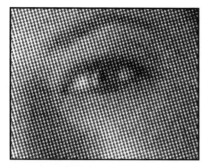

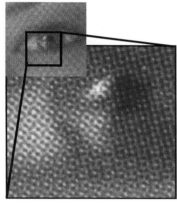

Here it is: ***Everything is printed in solid ink.*** A printing press cannot print in any other way. Solid ink: It's either inked, or it's not.

The top image on this page is a graphic that is an enlarged section of a black-and-white photo—called a "halftone" in the printing industry. It's all printed in black ink. You'd think it had shades of gray ink in it, but that's not the case. It is actually made up of tiny dots of varying size. It's the variation in the size of the dots and the apparent distance between them that determines how your eye sees the "shades of gray" they create. The brain puts them all together, and they look gray. Back off from the page and notice how the dots lose their individuality and the graphic becomes a collection of grays.

If you look at a "full-color photograph" in any magazine, you'll see the same kind of thing, but you'll see it in four colors. You'll see four patterns of dots: One set of variable-size, solid dots in the bluish *cyan,* one set in the pinkish *magenta*, one set in *yellow, and* one set in black. Each color is printed with its lines of dots at specific angles. Again, the brain puts them together, and they show as many colors.

Exception #1: In the world of inkjet printing (not used for web or sheet fed jobs), manufacturers have come up with more than four colors of ink in an attempt to create more precise color printing on the desktop. Some have up to seven ink colors, and some of the ink colors are "light black," "red," "green," and other colors. These aren't the standard four colors mentioned above, but they are still put on the paper as solid ink, placed in dots to simulate varying light and dark tones.

Exception #2: Inks for printing on presses can be created in colors other than the four standard colors, also. For many years, a company named Pantone has manufactured inks of every possible hue throughout the spectrum. These are known as "solid ink colors," and, like crayons in a box, they cover the gamut of colors. Their use is in printing a specific, repeatable color as a solid ink. It might be a light blue, a gray, a pink, or any other color. These inks are used on sheet fed and web presses, when called for by the print job. Pantone inks are designated by numbers. "PMS187c" means "Pantone Matching System #187 for coated paper," and it is always exactly the same shade of red when printed on coated papers, no matter who prints it.

Photos

A black-and-white photograph, in order to be printed by a printing press, must be converted to a dot pattern. This dot pattern is called a "halftone." The halftone is the graphic of the photo. (A photograph you get on photographic paper from a photo lab is a "continuous tone" image; look at it with the magnifying glass and you'll see no dots, just "continuous" tones, like "real life." You might *think* you see dots, but what you're seeing is often the grain structure of the photographic negative, which has layers of color dyes in the exact opposite color that you'll see on a well-made photographic print.)

If the photo is going to be printed in "full color," it must be "color separated." Full color means it tries to simulate real world colors. Color separated means that the real-world colors must be separated into the four printing colors, cyan, magenta, yellow and black, known as C,M,Y and K or just CMYK. (Each color is printed from a separate plate and roller assembly in the press.) The color separation process also produces a dot-pattern graphic of each color—a *halftone* in cyan, one in magenta, one in yellow, and one in black. When printed on paper, these four patterns of solid ink dots will combine to produce a close approximation of colors in our real world. (See the previous page, bottom image, for an example.) Look at any printed color image with a the magnifying glass and you'll see it.

To be complete: There *are* photos printed in two ink colors, called "duotones." Photos printed in three colors are called "tritones." Photos printed in four colors could be called "quadtones," but when they're printed so as to represent true colors of the world, they're just called "color photos" or "full color."

In general, though, the photos your magazines carry will be called "halftones" for black-and-white photo illustration, and "4-color," "full-color," or just "color" for color photo illustration.

We are *so* lucky in this high-tech age. Computer programs all take care of the color separations, instead of some guy with years of experience doing it by photographing a color print with a process camera and various color-eliminating filters! (A laborious task, and extremely expensive for printing. That's why my original magazines had only a color cover, and the interior was all black and white. Now, they're all full color, all the way through.)

Line Art

Any graphic that is printed not to look like a photo would normally be referred to as "line art." It simply means that the graphic is not a simulation of a real-world photograph. It is a solid body of ink. This box (■■■■■) is "line art." Solid ink, not a dot pattern.

Again, we are all so lucky, because we just do these things in a computer program and the computer takes care of it for us.

Although, in fact, a photographic halftone that is a pattern of solid dots is, strictly speaking, "line art," it is not referred to that way, but is referred to by the more specific term, "halftone." The distinction is made depending on how the art looks to the naked eye. If it is printed in black ink, and it looks like solid black and paper (ink or no ink), then it's most often called "line art."

In the real world, when people are talking about graphics, art, halftones, etc., and they know the items to which they're referring, they don't use these fancy terms all the time. They just call it art, or picture, or "that art in the upper left corner."

Applying These Terms To Computer Graphics

When computers came into wide use, and different companies began producing graphics programs, everything got easier and faster, but it also became more complex in some ways.

It got easier in the sense that you could now scan a photo or piece of art, process it some, and have it in the computer to place on your page. Or, you could create it in the computer program and save it on your disk. Or, you could buy a collection of graphics, in fact the same collections you used to buy in clip-art books.

It got more complex, though, in that several different "graphic formats" came into being. Some were designed for Windows computers, others for Macintosh. Some were for "paint" programs, and some were designed for "draw" programs. Those terms are hardly used anymore, although there are some software programs that are named with them, such as CorelDRAW and CorelPAINT.

Basically, *paint* programs are "bitmap" programs, creating art with "pixel maps," or "bit maps." Adobe Photoshop is one.

Basically, *draw* programs are "vector art" programs, creating art by recreating a mathematical formula that can render the art perfectly regardless of resolution of the output device—it looks perfect on a 72 or 96 pixel-per-inch monitor screen, or when output through a 2,560-line Linotronic Imagesetter. Adobe Illustrator is one.

Bitmapped Art

Technically, "bitmap art" is defined by "pixels." The higher number of "pixels per inch" you set when you create the art, the sharper it will be when printed. Pixels per inch, or ppi, is a measure of "resolution." (Also referred to as "dpi"—"dots per inch.")

What's "resolution?" The "resolution" of any art is the number of lines-per-inch, dots-per-inch, or pixels-per-inch at which it is created and saved. With bitmapped art, like that done in Photoshop, the LPI, DPI, or PPI *matters*. The way the art looks, when you print it, is *dependent* on the *resolution* at which you create it: It's called "resolution dependent."

Because of this limitation, you have to create the art at a resolution that will print clearly when you go to press. That's all. The basic rule you follow is this. Ask your printer the lpi value (lines per inch) at which they will print your magazine. No matter what they say, double it, and use that as the resolution for your bitmapped art—photos, lines, and everything. A simple formula.

For example, if your printing process is 133 lines per inch (a standard resolution for offset printing), create your bitmapped art (in a program like Photoshop) at twice that resolution. The dialog box you'll see won't have "lines per inch." It will show "pixels per inch." Use a figure twice the lines-per-inch figure your printer gave you—266 ppi, or for simplicity, make it 300 ppi. That will give you nice, sharp art at 133 lpi.

You can use even higher resolutions (such as 600 ppi) if you want the lines in your art to be absolutely perfect, even under a magnifying glass. (However, the files will be about four times larger with double the resolution.)

Our magazines are printed at 133 lines per inch; my art ("graphics") specifications call for at least a 300 line-per-inch original (computer art), whether the art, or graphic, is a scanned photograph or line art. This eliminates most jagged lines, though 600 lines per inch would do it better and look even smoother. (But a 600-line image takes up about four times as much space on disk as a 300-line image file.)

For photos, I just tell photographs to send them on a CD. Every pro-level digital camera used at weddings provides a file that can be interpolated to 300 dpi in Photoshop.

What You Do In Bitmap Programs

A bitmap program, like Photoshop, is used mostly for manipulation and control of photographic art, like halftones and color photos to be placed in the page layout program. Our full-color magazine covers are done in Photoshop because the program offers the manipulation we need of every element (type, line art, and photos). It also offers all the effects we want, such as drop shadows, glows, bevels, variable transparency of layers, and so forth.

Vector Art

"Vector Art," technically speaking, is art that is created by the computer from a mathematical formula. You draw a triangle on the screen with your mouse and cursor; the computer converts your lines into math. *Lots* of math. The math, then, when recreated on another computer (like when you send your disk to a printer and they put it into their computer), defines everything. It puts the lines where you put them, etc.

Whereas bitmap art, described above, was resolution *dependent*, Vector Art is *"resolution independent."* That means that if you create a triangle in a vector art program, like Adobe Illustrator or CorelDRAW, it will *never* have a stairstepped edge. You can even increase vector art's size to be much greater than the size at which you created it, and it won't develop jagged line edges. (The math does it.)

Vector art—being *resolution independent*. It has no "built-in" resolution. (For that reason, it's also referred to sometimes as "device dependent," printing at the output device's highest resolution.)

Graphics Programs

Adobe Illustrator and Adobe Photoshop both have the capability of creating combined vector art and bitmapped art in the same graphic file. This makes things a bit easier, but, the resolution factor still applies.

I like Photoshop. I no longer use Illustrator at all. The two basic programs I use are Adobe InDesign and Adobe Photoshop, and they do *everything* I need to do for the magazines or any other publications (such as this one, created in InDesign and exported as a PDF so you can read it easily online with Adobe Reader or Acrobat). I like the Adobe programs; they all work well together, and they are all available for Mac and Windows, making "cross-platform" almost a meaningless term for graphics.

COMPUTER GRAPHICS FORMATS

There are a number of standardized formats used in graphics. Four of them are used more often than all the others put together. They are PDF, TIF, JPG, and EPS. You can accept an ad in any of these formats and convert it to any other of them in Photoshop.

PDF (Adobe Acrobat Portable Document Format)

When Adobe brought out Acrobat PDF format ("Portable Document Format: :a post-script-based file format), many people just didn't "get it." As you probably know, a PDF reproduces, onscreen or for print, the page exactly as you lay it out in your own computer. PDFs are useful for all sorts of purposes, the *most* useful being the providing of a perfectly laid-out page to the printer, as you will do with your magazines.

This ebook or printed version is another good example. It was written and laid out in InDesign and simply exported (in File>Export) to a PDF. That PDF is what you're reading now. No printer involved, unless you print a copy for your own use on your own desktop printer. (Please remember the Copyright rules.)

You can take any page, any graphic, or any complete publication produced in a Post-script page layout program (like QuarkXPress or InDesign), and save or export it as a PDF. The PDF document can be tailored to its specific end-use: Screen viewing, low-resolution printing, high-resolution printing, an ebook like this one, etc. This PDF looks *exactly* like the original, with all of the graphics and type in the right places, perfectly reproduced.

Many a taxpayer, on April 15 at 7 pm, unable to get the tax form they need any other way, can simply go on the internet to **http://www.irs.gov** and get into the forms pages. There, they can download to their computer an original, perfect and approved IRS form that they can print on their own printer, fill out by hand, and include with their tax return.

That's the usefulness of PDF. It works not only for forms, but for "soft proofing" of all kinds of ads and of complete publications.

You are using it right now to read this document; this entire book was transmitted as a PDF.

A Suggested Workflow

I request that all ad graphics come to me as one of these files, in this order: PDF, TIF, EPS, or JPG. Most of them are in the RGB colorspace. When I receive the file, I open it in Photoshop. Then I convert the profile from whatever it originally was to Photoshop's built-in profile, SWOPv2, which means Standard Web Offset Printing, version 2. (It automatically converts an RGB file to the CMYK needed for printing.) Then I save it as a tif at 300 dpi, name it with the page number first (e.g. "79_RosesForYou.tif"), and put it in my "Ads" folder.

The ad is then placed in my publication where it's supposed to go.

It's a simple and easy workflow for each graphic element (ads *and* photos) in your publication. Here it is in numbered steps:

1) Receive CMYK or RGB Ad File (PDF, TIF, JPG or PSD) from advertiser.

2) Open Ad File in Photoshop.

3) In Image>Image Size: check/convert: Should be 300 dpi at correct ad dimensions

4) In Edit>Convert To Profile: Convert Profile from whatever it is, to SWOPv2 (Converts the image to CMYK for you; if not using a Web printer, use another profile.)

5) Sharpen if necessary, change color balance if necessary, edit if necessary

6) Save as a TIF image, no compression.

7) Name by page number in a separate directory/folder for easy reference. (This will also leave the original file intact -- a good thing.)

Done.

NOTE: This is exactly the same procedure you follow with each photo to be placed in the publication. It can easily be automated using Photoshop's "Actions" function.

This Chapter Has Barely Scratched The Surface

Though there is more to know about this subject, you'll find that much of it will be "taught" to you by your computer programs. If I were to make just one strong suggestion that would make your life easier as a publisher, it would be this: Buy Adobe Photoshop and learn it. It does everything in the graphics realm that you will ever need done.

In addition to it, you'll need your page layout program, and you'll want the *full* version of Adobe Acrobat (not just Reader, which you can get for free get on the internet). With just those three programs, you can publish high-quality magazines.

Why The tax Form in This Particular Chapter?

Only because it is an Adobe PDF and it's there to illustrate the accuracy of the file format. But, you probably already knew that since PDF is the format of this book!

SCHEDULE C
(Form 1040)

Department of the Treasury
Internal Revenue Service (99)

Profit or Loss From Business
(Sole Proprietorship)

▶ Partnerships, joint ventures, etc., generally must file Form 1065 or 1065-B.
▶ Attach to Form 1040, 1040NR, or 1041.   ▶ See Instructions for Schedule C (Form 1040).

OMB No. 1545-0074

2008

Attachment
Sequence No. **09**

Name of proprietor

Social security number (SSN)

A	Principal business or profession, including product or service (see page C-3 of the instructions)	**B** Enter code from pages C-9, 10, & 11 ▶
C	Business name. If no separate business name, leave blank.	**D** Employer ID number (EIN), if any
E	Business address (including suite or room no.) ▶ _____ City, town or post office, state, and ZIP code	

F Accounting method: **(1)** ☐ Cash   **(2)** ☐ Accrual   **(3)** ☐ Other (specify) ▶ _____
G Did you "materially participate" in the operation of this business during 2008? If "No," see page C-4 for limit on losses   ☐ Yes ☐ No
H If you started or acquired this business during 2008, check here   . . . . ▶ ☐

Part I   Income

1	Gross receipts or sales. **Caution.** See page C-4 and check the box if: • This income was reported to you on Form W-2 and the "Statutory employee" box on that form was checked, or • You are a member of a qualified joint venture reporting only rental real estate income not subject to self-employment tax. Also see page C-4 for limit on losses. . . ▶ ☐	**1**
2	Returns and allowances	**2**
3	Subtract line 2 from line 1	**3**
4	Cost of goods sold (from line 42 on page 2)	**4**
5	**Gross profit.** Subtract line 4 from line 3.	**5**
6	Other income, including federal and state gasoline or fuel tax credit or refund (see page C-4).	**6**
7	**Gross income.** Add lines 5 and 6 . . . . ▶	**7**

Part II   Expenses. Enter expenses for business use of your home **only** on line 30.

8	Advertising	**8**	18	Office expense	**18**
9	Car and truck expenses (see page C-5).	**9**	19	Pension and profit-sharing plans	**19**
10	Commissions and fees . .	**10**	20	Rent or lease (see page C-6):	
11	Contract labor (see page C-5)	**11**	a	Vehicles, machinery, and equipment	**20a**
12	Depletion	**12**	b	Other business property . .	**20b**
13	Depreciation and section 179 expense deduction (not included in Part III) (see page C-5)	**13**	21	Repairs and maintenance . .	**21**
			22	Supplies (not included in Part III)	**22**
			23	Taxes and licenses . . .	**23**
			24	Travel, meals, and entertainment:	
			a	Travel	**24a**
14	Employee benefit programs (other than on line 19) .	**14**	b	Deductible meals and entertainment (see page C-7)	**24b**
15	Insurance (other than health) .	**15**	25	Utilities	**25**
16	Interest:		26	Wages (less employment credits) .	**26**
a	Mortgage (paid to banks, etc.) .	**16a**	27	Other expenses (from line 48 on page 2)	**27**
b	Other	**16b**			
17	Legal and professional services	**17**			

28	**Total expenses** before expenses for business use of home. Add lines 8 through 27 . . . . ▶	**28**
29	Tentative profit or (loss). Subtract line 28 from line 7	**29**
30	Expenses for business use of your home. Attach **Form 8829**	**30**
31	**Net profit or (loss).** Subtract line 30 from line 29. • If a profit, enter on both **Form 1040, line 12,** and **Schedule SE, line 2,** or on **Form 1040NR, line 13** (if you checked the box on line 1, see page C-7). Estates and trusts, enter on **Form 1041, line 3.** • If a loss, you **must** go to line 32.	**31**
32	If you have a loss, check the box that describes your investment in this activity (see page C-8). • If you checked 32a, enter the loss on both **Form 1040, line 12,** and **Schedule SE, line 2,** or on **Form 1040NR, line 13** (if you checked the box on line 1, see the line 31 instructions on page C-7). Estates and trusts, enter on **Form 1041, line 3.** • If you checked 32b, you **must** attach **Form 6198.** Your loss may be limited.	**32a** ☐ All investment is at risk. **32b** ☐ Some investment is not at risk.

For Paperwork Reduction Act Notice, see page C-9 of the instructions.   Cat. No. 11334P   Schedule C (Form 1040) 2008

Ah, TAXES! At least, this is one form you will want to fill out in as much legitimate deductible detail as you can. It is shown here because it is a PDF, reduced, but perfect.

Chapter 19

MAKING PHOTOS LOOK GOOD IN PRINT

Though photographic art was discussed briefly in the previous chapter, photos deserve more space.

Photos give realism and immediacy to your publication. They illustrate like no graphic art can. They can show the good, bad and ugly—when they, themselves, are reproduced well. If they are not reproduced well, nobody sees the "good."

In order for a photograph to print well, whether it's grayscale or color, it must have two properties: Detail in the shadows, and detail in the highlights.

In the national magazines, you normally see only photos with those two requirements. They are reproduced well, with detail in shadows and highlights.

Walk over to the rack where the "freebies" are: You know, the real estate magazines and the senior citizen tabloids. Browse through their photos, and you'll see many with washed out highlights and dark, blocked-up shadows. They did not reproduce well, but they could have, if they had been processed correctly before being placed on the publication page.

What does good photo "processing" in the computer consist of? Here's a primer.

What Ink Does When Pressed Onto Paper

Why do we use tissue to blow our noses instead of regular paper? You have fifteen seconds to guess. Please don't spend the whole time thinking, "what a ridiculous question and what could he possibly be getting at?"

(Jeopardy theme plays … .) … … …   Time's up.

It's because tissue is more absorbent. Its fibers are farther apart and looser than those of regular paper.

Car detailers all know that the most effective paper for washing car windows is a newspaper. (Another reason your advertisers should invest ad money in your magazines instead of the daily paper!) Newspapers, or "newsprint" as the paper itself is generally called, are just absorbent enough to use for the purpose. And, the ink in the paper helps to polish the glass.

Can you imagine using the glossy pages of a coffee table book to wash windows? Putting the issue of wasting a nice book aside, the paper wouldn't soak up the window washing fluid very well, would it?

Here's the point of all this silliness: *Paper's absorbency directly affects how your images look on it.* To look at it from the printer's point of view, different papers "hold ink out" differently. Holding ink out, on the surface of the paper, keeps it from soaking into the paper and spreading among the fibers.

A simple office stamp shows the difference: Tissue below, coated paper above. Consider your paper when processing photos. Ink expands on paper, filling the area between dots. It shows more on uncoated paper, less on coated paper.

Ink is a liquid. When it is mashed onto a paper surface, it goes in and spreads as it is absorbed. When it spreads in the fibers of the paper and on the surface of the paper, it gets just a little bit bigger. This is called "dot gain," and it does more to ruin more photos in publications than anything else.

Remember that a "halftone" or a "full color photo" are both printed on paper as solid dots of inks? A black-and-white halftone is printed of dots of black ink. In the lightest highlights, the dots are extremely small, with lots of space in between them. In the darkest shadows, the dots are large, with not much space between them. In the middle tone areas, the dots and the space between them are about the same.

When the dots in the dark shadow areas "gain" in size, since there isn't much space between them, the amount of extra width they gain because of spreading in and on the paper reduces the space between them. This darkens that area. If they gain enough "weight" to completely fill up the space, the shadow turns totally black, and there is no detail.

This happens to varying degrees throughout all the tones of the photo. The lights, mids and darks all get darker when the ink hits the paper. The more absorbent the paper, the darker they all appear

This occurs with all papers and with all inks of every color.

The amount of weight a dot of ink "gains" on paper can be quantified as a percentage. Part of it has to do with the color and type of ink. But the biggest part has to do with the paper the ink lands on.

There is a simple solution to this: Your printer will tell you how much "dot gain" to allow for. If he tells you to expect about a 20% dot gain (an average amount) then you will know exactly how to set your the program to compensate. (The compensation, which is done automatically, actually reduces the dot size in the halftone so that, when it expands on the paper, it will become the size it needs to be for correct tonality. Ta-da!)

In Photoshop, if you want to, you can manually set the value of dot gain for grayscale images (black-and-white photos) at several different percentages. For most glossy magazine papers, a 95% shadow value and 5% highlight value works well, and lightening the middle value by about 3% to 5% will also provide more middle-tone detail. (These are set in the Image>Adjustments>Curves dialog box. The "black" and "white" points can be set automatically if you wish, but the middle-tone point must be set manually.) For color images, Adobe Photoshop's profiling will set the gain percentage for you.

It is easier than it sounds, once you get into it.

Shadow Value, Highlight Value, and Middle Tones

Many photographic prints have a pure white and a pure black in them. However, in order for these to print correctly, the white areas must have *some* dots in them, and the black areas must have *some* open paper between their dots. This makes the tones, or tonal values, of the photo look right when printed. Even objects in the very deep shadows can display some detail. This is how we see in "real life," and 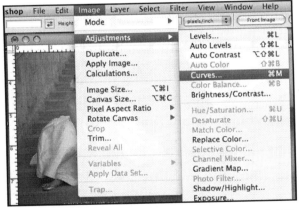 if we don't see objects about the same way in printed photos, the don't look natural. We expect to see detail in shadows and gradual shadow/highlight transitions throughout.

The Photoshop Curves Box

In Photoshop, with a grayscale image, you can easily determine the tonal values of any grayscale image in one little dialog box: The Image>Adjustments>Curves box. A "curve" is a graph representing the tones in the picture, from black (100%) at the top right to white (0%) at the bottom left. (See next page.)

Highlight Value:
You can grab the ends of the line on the graph and move them. By moving the left bottom end (the whites), clicking and holding it, and dragging it up the left side of the box, you can make it so that the two little number boxes (input and output) show you "input-0" and "output-5%." This will give you a

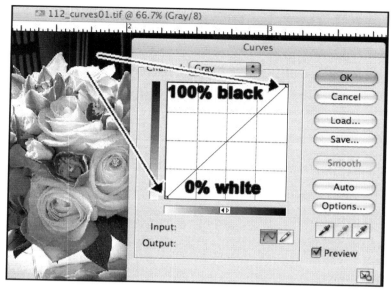

5% dot in the pure white areas; they'll still look white to the eye, but they'll have some texture. On the screen, as you do this, you'll see the highlights in the photo get just a little bit grayer.

Shadow Value:
Now, at the top right corner of the box, (the blacks), you can grab the end of the graph line and drag it down the right side of the box, so that the Input is 100%, and the output is 95%.

In the illustration at right, the Input/Output boxes reflect the middle tones: A 50% mid tone will print a 45%.

If you compare the photos in both boxes above, you can see even on your computer screen that the reproduction of the bottom photo will be more realistic and pleasing to the eye, with its 5%-45%-95% settings.

Just ask your printer this question: "What are the highlight and shadow settings I should use?" (They are sometimes called the "black point and white point.") My printer told me, since I use glossy paper, to set a 95% shadow and a 5% highlight. So, I make the solid blacks into 95% black, and the solid whites into 5% white. With the lightening of middle tones of up to 5%, the result is excellent, as you'll see if you purchase a sample set of my magazines. (See the web page: **www.WriteAMagazine.com**.)

Your printer might say, if you're printing on newsprint, "Use a 75% shadow and a 5% highlight." You create these settings in Photoshop, for each photo, the same way as described above. The photo will look grayish and "washed out" on your screen and in your laser or inkjet proof copy, but don't worry: It has to be this way because you must compensate for "dot gain" on the soft, uncoated newsprint paper. (Laser prints, and inkjet prints to a lesser degree, don't display dot gain in the same way as offset printing, which uses liquid inks.)

You can pinpoint a spot on your photo and have a "point" appear on your graph line in Photoshop. You do this by holding down the "Apple" or Command key on the Mac keyboard and clicking on the photo; Windows has a similar keystroke.

Because I deal with Brides, I've often chosen light facial areas as my adjustment point. For untanned Caucasian skin, a soft highlight tone should be from 18% to 22%. For Black skin, the same kind of highlight area should be from 26% to 40%. For tanned Caucasian or Medium Hispanic skin, the same highlight should be about 22% to 24%. And so forth.

(Numbers in the above paragraphs are a good guideline, but the settings I use might not necessarily be the settings you use. However, the basic necessity of setting black and white points is a standard adjustment in all halftones, or black and white, photos.)

If you have a problem with all of this, ask the printer to send or show you some printed samples on the same paper you'll use. When you see a photo whose overall tones you like, call or visit your contact at the printing company and ask about the shadow tones, the highlight tones, the middle tones, and other values discussed above. Use the answers you get as a starting point for similar photographs. They will print your job as they receive it, unless you pay them to fix it. (It's expensive.) But, they want your job to look as good as possible; if it does, you're more likely to continue using their services.

Color Photos

The automatic profile set in Photoshop is so good that not as much adjustment is required of color photos as of halftones. However, if you aren't dealing with pro photographers, you might need to make more drastic adjustments.

Chapter 20

PRODUCTION: PUTTING IT ALL TOGETHER

Ta-Da!

Congratulations! It's time for you to put it all together. Let's recap what's been done so far.

Sales

You've sold, and/or your salesperson has sold, enough ads to publish your first edition. This might be at a profit or simply a break-even point (which is what I shoot for in my first editions).

You had set aside room in your Preview Edition for 104 one-card ad spaces, and you ended up selling 89. The required ad space leaves some nice, open layout room, and you're anxious to get it all on the pages.

Text

You or someone has written original text for every article. The only things left are a couple of date-sensitive schedules for trade shows that you want to get at the last minute.

You've proofread the text, and it's all just right. The tone and style are casual, informative, entertaining and direct. It's just right for your audience.

Graphics

You have a few graphics that fit your subject, all from legal sources, or from copyright owners who have granted permission in writing to use them. Other graphics, that you've created or taken from graphics collections you've purchased, you have saved on your hard disk as EPS or TIF files, and they are ready to place in the pages of your publication

Ad Graphics

The ads have arrived on time (for the most part). Some of them came in by email, others by special delivery at the last minute, and others were here far in advance of the deadline. Anyway, there are only a couple of ads still outstanding, and you're confident they'll get here. In any case, you know where they go and their size, so you can just leave the room needed for them in the layout. That's the basic situation I'm usually in at this point.

THE PRODUCTION WORKFLOW

"Production" is the process of taking those bits of text and art and putting them all together on your pages, polishing it, proofreading it, and packaging it for the printer. It's not complicated.

Start The "Real" Layout

Here's some good news: Since you already created the entire magazine for your Preview Edition, you won't have to rebuild it from the ground up. Most of it has already been done. The production of an entire new publication is only a three-week process.(And, yes, you *do* get to take the weekends off!)

Adapt The Preview Edition

First, make a duplicate of the Preview Edition file. Your original Preview Edition should now be named something "original_preview" so that you'll have it as a reference and backup. Besides, you'll be using it again in its Preview Edition form if you publish a second edition in a nearby (or faraway) location.

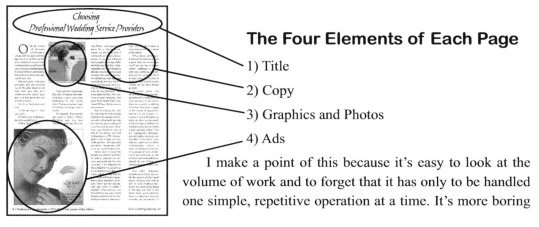

The Four Elements of Each Page

1) Title

2) Copy

3) Graphics and Photos

4) Ads

I make a point of this because it's easy to look at the volume of work and to forget that it has only to be handled one simple, repetitive operation at a time. It's more boring than difficult!

I separate the ads and graphics as items just to keep them organized in my own mind. I also separate them into their own folders in the computer for the same reason. (Refer back to page 44.) Technically, ads and photos would be called "graphics," and there is no reason why they couldn't be put into the same folder. But for me, it works best to separate them.

A Step-by-Step Process

The conversion of those four elements from the preview edition into their "real" versions in the finished publication is not hard, since everything is ready to go. I do it in this order, having found through the years that this works best in my situation.

1) Your titles will probably be changed, reworded, or done in a different type font.

2) Your real copy will replace your Greek, and you'll do some copy fitting.

3) Your graphics and photos will replace empty boxes, and probably be resized.

4) Your ads will replace empty ad grid boxes, with page layouts probably changing.

Photo Selection and Editing

It is normally at this very late point when I actually make my photo selections from the photographs sent to me by advertisers. Why do I wait?

Procrastination! (Not mine, but that of the photographers and advertisers!)

Human nature being what it is, some advertisers send photographs early in the process (just as some send ads early). Others (most of them, actually) wait until the very latest possible moment, and then they don't put them in the mail until the day they were supposed to be on my desk. (One year, before email became as widely used as it is now, I counted up over $400 worth of FedEx, UPS and USPS overnight envelopes people used in the last couple of days because they had procrastinated. Such a waste.)

So that I will know that I have given the advertisers every possible chance to get the photos to me for the publication, I wait a week after the final deadline before I start selecting.

How do I select?

It's pretty high-tech: You see, I have a ping-pong table in my basement. I print a copy of my Working Final Edition (with empty photo boxes on the pages), with final ad spots marked, real text inserted, and everything where it will really be at the end.

I take all the photos, and I spread them out on the ping-pong table, each in a marked stack (usually by stacking them on top of the envelope they came in). I look through every one of them once or twice so I'll have a general Idea of what is available, and then I start selecting.

For an article on Choosing Wedding Professionals, for example, I'll use a photo of a photographer photographing, or a caterer catering or a musician playing. I simply choose the best photo I have available that fits the subject matter of the article. This would be the same procedure regardless of the subject of the magazine.

I mark photos with a Sharpie marker, on the back of the photo. The Sharpie dries fast, doesn't bleed through, and does not damage the image in any way. I mark it on the reverse side of a dark area of the photo. (Why I use Sharpie: A ball point will leave an impression; a pencil does the same. A gel pen will smudge.)

If a page, say page number 31, has one photo, the photo and the space will both be marked "31-A." If there are two photos, the second one will be 31-B, and so forth.

I proceed all the way through the magazine, then, keeping each advertiser's photos together, take them back up to my office and start scanning. It doesn't take long to process fifty or sixty photos—a couple of hours or so.

But, That's How I Used To Do It ... Now, it's Different

It could be done that way, but it isn't anymore. For the last two years (2008 and 2009 editions), I have received photos only digitally — either on CD or DVD, or downloaded from a website. I don't own the ping-pong table anymore.

Now, I receive many more photos than I used to receive. Where I once got about 800 to 1,000 prints to consider from 15 to 20 photographers, I now have to go through from 10,000 to 15,000. They send them all on CDs and DVDs (sometimes multiples), and, searching for the perfect cover photo, I look at every one of them. Quickly.

Here's how I like to do it, by way of suggestion. First, I copy the entire CD or DVD onto my computer's internal drive to speed up the process.

2009 Cover

Having done that and named each folder of photos for the photographer ("Jones2009," etc.), I scan through the photos in my Mac's "Coverflow" option, which displays thumbnails very speedily. When I see a promising candidate for either the cover or for use inside the magazine (for which I'll need from 80 to 120 photos), I drag it into another folder, appropriately named something like "Jones2009-faves." After I've looked through all of Jones's many submissions and those I like in the "faves" folder, I'll throw away the original "Jones-2009" folder. I don't need it anymore, since I have the originals on the CDs or DVDs if I want to see them again. Then, I pick photos for use only from the respective "faves" folder of all the photographers.

After I finish selecting photos for the "faves" folders, I will turn to the task of converting from the Preview Master pages to the Final Master pages.

Create Your Final Master Page

A "Final Master" can be used to replace each of the other master pages as you work through the magazine.

Create one new Left and Right Master Page set, and name it "Final Master," or some-

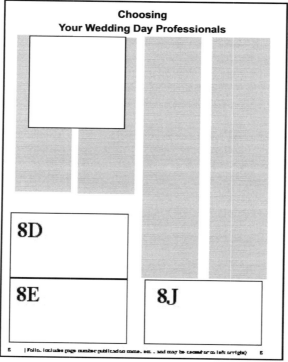

thing to that effect. Then, if you've created it by duplicating another R/L Master page, just remove all of the items on it except the folio (the page number and magazine edition information at the botom of the page). On the Final Master Page, reword the folio to say anything you want. Then you can simply open the magazine page you're working on and replace the Preview Edition Master Page, like the one on the left (previous page) into a page like the one on the right—with no ad place-holders (boxes with position numbers). Then you can drop in the "real" elements that belong on the final page. It will save you time because your major designing of the page has already been done; you just repeat it.

Process Sections As They Close

Some pages and sections of your magazine will "close" before others do.

While your remaining ad sales are being made, you can shortcut the overall production time by processing those closed pages.

For the examples on the next few pages, imagine that pages 2 through 5 of our magazine are finished: The ads that will sell on them have been sold. We can start finalizing those pages anytime we want.

On the next few pages are thumbnails of pages 2 through 5 of one of my *Wedding & Party Magazine* editions. The complete PDF of this 40-page plus-cover edition is available at my website: **www.WriteAMagazine.com**.

The thumbnails shown follow the step above, that is, after substituting the new Final Master for the Preview Master Pages.

Page 120: Set Up Frames or Boxes For Photos and Graphics

Having placed boxes for the ad spaces exactly where they are supposed to go, you now have some major elements in place. The page is built around the ad positions already sold.

Open your publication so that you can see all of a two-page spread on your computer screen. Play with it a bit. You want the layout of the spread to have a clear flow of information and to be pleasing to the eye. (The requirement isn't "high art"; it is clear communication within a layout that doesn't detract from the information.) Put in some boxes (frames) for photos. Move them around, change their sizes, etc., until you can see a nice balance and flow to the two-page spread. When you are happy with it, go to the next step. In time, you'll find that you can do this very quickly.

Text Continued on page 123

PREVIEW EDITION PAGES 2-5: Ads & Photos Blocked; Text In

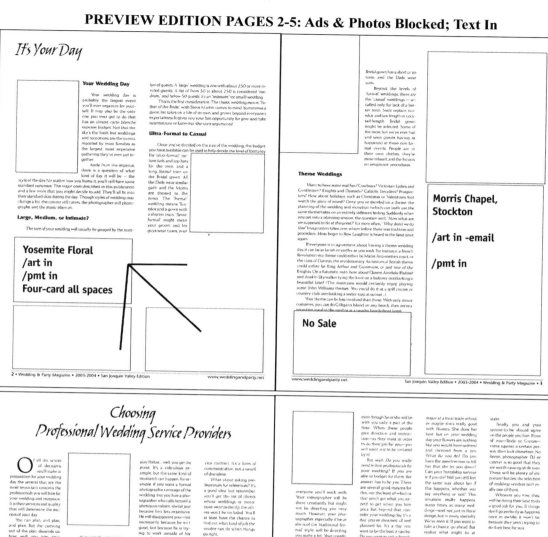

It's Your Day

Your Wedding Day

Your wedding day is probably the largest event you'll ever organize for yourself. It may also be the only one you ever get to do that has an almost carte blanche expense budget. Not that the sky's the limit; but weddings and receptions are the events reported by most families as the largest, most expensive gathering they've ever put together.

Aside from the expense, there is a question of what kind of day it will be -- the style of the day. No matter how you frame it, you'll still have some standard extremes. The major ones described in this publication and a few more that you might decide to add. They'll all fit into their standard slots during the day. Though styles of wedding may change a bit, the caterer still caters, the photographer still photographs, and the music plays on.

Large, Medium, or Intimate?

The size of your wedding will usually be gauged by the number of guests. A 'large' wedding is one with about 250 or more invited guests. A list of from 50 to about 250 is considered 'medium,' and below 50 guests it's an 'intimate' or small wedding.

This is the first consideration. The classic wedding movie 'Father of the Bride,' with Steve Martin comes to mind. Sometimes a guest list takes on a life of its own and grows beyond everyone's expectations. It gives you your first opportunity for give-and-take negotiations or katti-but-the-door arguments!

Ultra-Formal to Casual

Once you've decided on the size of the wedding, the budget you have available can be used to help decide the level of formality for 'ultra-formal,' picture tails and top hats for the men, and a long, formal train on the Bridal gown. All the Dads wear similar garb, and the Moms are dressed to the nines. The 'formal' wedding means 'tuxedos and a gown with a shorter train. 'Semi-formal' might mean your groom and his guys wear tuxes, your

Yosemite Floral
/art in
/pmt in
Four-card all spaces

Bridal gown has a sheet or no train, and the Dads wear suits.

Beyond the levels of formal weddings, there are the 'casual' weddings -- so-called only for lack of a better term. Suits replace tuxedos and tea-length or cocktail-length Bridal gown might be selected. Some of the most fun we've ever had and seen guests having is happened at these non-formal events. People are in their own clothes, they're more relaxed, and the focus is on people not procedures.

Theme Weddings

Want to have some real fun? Cowboys? Victorian Ladies and Gentlemen? Knights and Damsels? Galactic Invaders? Prospectors? How about holidays, such as Christmas or Valentines (but watch the price of roses)? Once you've decided on a theme the planning of the wedding and reception (which can both use the same theme) takes on an entirely different feeling. Suddenly when you get into a planning session, the question isn't 'Now what are we supposed to do at this point?' It's more often, 'Why don't we do this?' Imagination takes over where before there was tradition and procedure. Ideas begin to flow. Laughter is heard in the land once again.

If everyone is in agreement about having a theme wedding day it can be as lavish or earthy as you wish. For instance a French Revolution-era theme could either be Marie Antoinettes court, or the class of Danton, the revolutionary. An historical British theme could either be King Arthur and Guinevere, or just one of the Knights. On a futuristic note, how about Queen Amidala (Padme) and Anakin Skywalker tying the knot on a balcony overlooking a beautiful lake? (The musicians would certainly enjoy playing some John Williams themes. You could do it at a golf course or country club overlooking a water-trap at sunset...)

Your theme can be less involved than these. With only minor costumes, you can do Gilligan's Island on any beach, then serve a reception meal in the sand or at a nearby beach-front hotel.

No Sale

Morris Chapel, Stockton

/art in -email

/pmt in

Choosing Professional Wedding Service Providers

Of all the scores of decisions you'll make in preparation for your wedding day, the several that are the most important concern the professionals you will hire for your wedding and reception. It is their services and quality that will determine the success of your day.

You can plan, and plan, and plan. But the carrying out of the plan depends on how well you hire pros whose services match your plan and how good they are at their services.

So, it's a three step process:
1: Decide exactly what you want
2: Find some professionals who can deliver it
3: Hire the best ones

If you get the impression that the success of the wedding day is up to you, from beginning to end, you're right. This is a pragmatic way of looking at things, and it works.

For example, if you decide you want a Polish Theme Wedding and hire Mariachis and ask them to play Polkas... well you get the point. It's a ridiculous example, but the same kind of mismatch can happen, for example, if you want a formal photographic coverage of the wedding but you hire a photographer who calls himself a 'photojournalist-style' just because he's less expensive. He will disappoint you--not necessarily because he isn't good, but because he is trying to work outside of his area of specialization. The same goes for the other services in your wedding. You want French food? Don't hire Good Ol' Boys Barbecues as your caterer.

Part of making the right decision also revolves around talking to the people or person who will actually provide services for your wedding. If you hire a DJ for your reception, you should be able to talk to the person who will be loading the CDs. This applies to all of your services: Videography, photography, ceremony musicians, celebrant, etc. It just makes sense.

When you've found the people you believe will best be able to provide the services you want, ask for their contract. A lot depends on their reliability as a business

vice contract. It is a form of communication, not a sword of discipline.

What about asking professionals for references? It's a good idea but remember you'll get the list of clients whose weddings or receptions went perfectly. The ones won't be included. You'll at least have the chance to find out what kind of job the vendor can do when things go right.

In many cases, you should be talking to the person who will actually provide your services. If you aren't, there is no point in talking. Of course, this doesn't apply to the rental of equipment, banquet rooms, or your ceremony location. It might not apply to other services such as floral design or balloon art, but there are a few to which it does strongly apply. They are videography, photography, disc jockey services, any provider of live music, your officiant, and your coordinator/consultant. Many of these wedding services hire extra people to meet the demand, you will want to talk to the person who will be assigned to you before you commit to a particular company.

Maciel & Co Jewelers

/art in

/pmt in

No Sale

everyone you'll work with. Your videographer will be there constantly, but might not be directing you very much. However, your photographer especially if he or she is of the 'traditional-formal' style, will be directing you quite a bit. Your coordinator will be with you from start to finish. If you like your officiant, you will have a better memory of the ceremony.

even though he or she will be with you quite a part of the time. When these people give direction and instructions--as they must in order to do their job for you--you will want not to be restated by it!

But wait. Do you really need to hire professionals for your wedding? If you are able to budget for them the answer has to be yes. There are several good reasons for this, not the least of which is that you'll get what you expect to get when you hire pros. But, beyond that, consider your wedding day. It's a day you've dreamed of and planned for. It's a day you want to be the best it can be. Do you want to risk a friendship over it? Imagine that your best friend says she will 'do your flowers' for you. Maybe she's a floral designer or maybe she's really good with flowers. She does her best day your flowers are nothing like you would have ordered and received from a pro. What do you do? Do you have the assertiveness to tell her that she let you down? Can your friendship survive if you do? Will you still feel the same way about her if this happens whether you say anything or not? This situation really happens many times, at many wedding--and not just in floral design, but in every specialty. We've seen it. If you want to take a chance go ahead. But realize what might be at

major at a local trade school, or maybe she's really good with flowers. She does her best day your flowers are nothing like you would have ordered and received from a pro.

stake.

Finally, you and your spouse-to-be should agree on the people you hire. If one of your--Bride or Groom--votes against a certain person, then look elsewhere. No florist, photographer, DJ or caterer is so good that they are worth causing strife over. There will be plenty of important battles the selection of wedding vendors isn't really one of them.

Whoever you hire, they will be doing their best to do a good job for you. It things don't go perfectly as happens once in awhile, it won't be because they aren't trying to do their best for you.

Ramada Inn Mission de Oro

/art in

/pmt in

No Sale

PREVIEW EDITION PAGES 2-5: Ads Blocked; Text In and Photos In

It's Your Day

Your Wedding Day

Your wedding day is probably the largest event you'll ever organize for yourself. It may also be the only one you ever get to do that has an almost carte blanche expense budget. Not that the sky's the limit, but weddings and receptions are the events reported by most families as the largest, most expensive gathering they've ever put together.

Aside from the expense, there is a question of what kind of day it will be — the style of the day. No matter how you frame it, you'll still have some standard expenses. The major ones described in this publication and a few more that you might decide to add. They'll all fit into their standard slots during the day. Though styles of wedding may change a bit, the caterer still caters, the photographer still photographs, and the music plays on.

Large, Medium, or Intimate?

The size of your wedding will usually be gauged by the number of guests. A 'large' wedding is one with about 250 or more invited guests. A list of from 50 to about 250 is considered 'medium,' and below 50 guests, it's an 'intimate' (or small) wedding.

Ultra-Formal to Casual

Once you've decided on the size of the wedding, the budget you have available can be used to help decide the level of formality for 'ultra-formal,' particular tails and top hats for the men, and a long, formal train on the Bridal gown. All the Dads wear similar garb, and the Moms are dressed to the nines. The 'formal' wedding means Tuxedos and a gown with a shorter train. 'Semiformal' might mean your groom and his guys wear tuxes, your

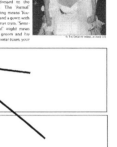

Bridal gown has a short or no train and the Dads wear suits.

Beyond the levels of 'formal' weddings there are the 'casual' weddings — so-called only for lack of a better term. Suits replace tuxedos and tea-length or cocktail-length Bridal gown might be selected. Some of the most fun we've ever had and seen guests having as happened at these non-formal events. People are in their own clothes, they're more relaxed, and the focus is on people not procedures.

Theme Weddings

Want to have some real fun? Cowboys? Victorian Ladies and Gentlemen? Knights and Damsels? Galactic Invaders? Prospectors? How about holidays, such as Christmas or Valentines that watch the price of cards? Once you've decided on a theme, the planning of the wedding and reception which can both use the same themed takes on an entirely different feeling. Suddenly when you get into a planning session, the question isn't, 'Now what are we supposed to do at this point?' It's more often, 'Why don't we do this?' Imagination takes over where before there was tradition and procedure. Ideas begin to flow. Laughter is heard in the land once again.

If everyone is in agreement about having a theme wedding, it can be as lavish or earthy as you wish. For instance, a French Revolution-era theme could either be Marie Antoinette's court, or the class of Danton, the revolutionary. At historical British theme could either be King Arthur and Guinevere, or just one of the Knights. On a futuristic note, how about Queen Amidala Padmé and Anakin Skywalker tying the knot on a balcony overlooking a beautiful lake? (The musicians would certainly enjoy playing some John Williams themes. You could do it at a golf course or country club overlooking a water-trap at sunset ...)

Your theme can be less involved than these. With only minor costumes, you can do Gilligan's Island on any beach, then serve a primitive meal in the sand or at a nearby beach front hotel.

How This Publication Is Organized

Regarding your search for wedding day services, you might want to consider interviewing for them in a certain order. Consider videography. The majority of weddings have a professional videographer. And not all videographers' results are the same.

Here's the rub: A specific videographer's work, that you might like, can't be done by anyone else. It's a personal set of skills, talent and technical expertise. The point is, if you want this person, you need to hire him or her for your wedding before someone else does!

So this publication is organized around the principle First Things First. Don't scan the major services you want because you're consumed with minor things. But, you should nail down the most limited services (e.g. locations, photography, videography, catering, music). Don't miss the Reception hall you like because you were listening to CDs to choose the tune for your first married dance!

If you go through the Contents and then our articles, you'll see that the organization is based on booking those services and products first that might not be there later.

Choosing Professional Wedding Service Providers

Of all the scores of decisions you'll make in preparation for your wedding day, the several that are the most important concern the professionals you will hire for your wedding and reception. It is their services and quality that will determine the success of your day.

You can plan and plan and plan. But, the carrying out of the plan depends on how well you hire pro's whose services match your plan, and how good they are at their services.

So, it's a three step process.

1) Decide exactly what you want

2) Find some professionals who can deliver it.

3) Hire the best ones.

If you get the impression that the success of the wedding day is up to you, from beginning to end, you're right. This is a pragmatic way of looking at things and it works.

For example, if you decide you want a Polish Theme Wedding, and you hire Mariachis and ask them to play Polkas , well you get the point. It's a ridiculous example but the same kind of mismatch can happen, for example, if you want a formal photographic coverage of the wedding, but you hire a photographer who calls himself a photojournalistic stylist just because he's less expensive. He will disappoint you—not necessarily because he isn't good, but because he is trying to work outside of his area of specialization. The same goes for the other services in your wedding. You want French food? Don't hire Good Ol' Boys Barbecue as your caterer.

Part of making the right decision also revolves around talking to the people or person who will actually provide services for your wedding. If you hire a DJ for your reception, you should be sure to talk to the person who will be loading the CDs. This applies to all of your services: Videography, photography, ceremony musicians, officiant, etc. It just makes sense.

When you've found the people you believe will best be able to provide the services you want, ask for their contract. A lot depends on

vice contract. It's a form of communication, not a sword of discipline.

What about asking professionals for references? It's a good idea, but remember, you'll get the list of clients whose weddings or receptions went perfectly; the others won't be included. You'll at least have the chance to find out what kind of job the vendor can do when things go right.

In many cases, you should be talking to the person who will actually provide your services, if you aren't, there is no point in talking. Of course, this doesn't apply to the rental of equipment, banquet rooms, or your ceremony location. It might not apply to other services such as floral design or balloon art, but there are a few to which it does strongly apply. They are videographers, photographers, disc jockey services, any provider of live music, your officiant, and your coordinator/consultant. Many of these wedding services here extra people to meet the demand: you will want to talk to the person who will be assigned to you before you commit to a particular com-

everyone you'll work with. Your videographer will be there constantly but might not be directing you very much. However your photographers, especially if he or she is of the 'traditional-formal' style, will be directing you quite a lot. Your coordinator will be with you from start to finish. If you like your officiant, you will have a better memory of the ceremony

even though, he or she will be with you only a part of the time. When these people give direction and instruction—as they must in order to do their job for you—you will want not to be irritated by it!

But wait. Do you really need to hire professionals for your wedding? If you are able to badger, by them the answer has to be yes. There are several good reasons for this, not the least of which is that you'll get what you expect. So to get when you hire pros. But, beyond that, consider your wedding day. It's a day you've dreamed of and planned for. It's a day you want to be the best it can be. Do you want to risk a friendship over it? Imagine that your best friend says she will do your flowers for you. Maybe she's a floral design

major at a local trade school or maybe she's really good with flowers. She does her best, but on your wedding day your flowers are nothing like you would have ordered and received from a pro. What do you do? Do you have the assertiveness to tell her that she let you down? Can your friendship survive it if you do? Will you still feel the same way about her if this happens, whether you say anything or not? These situation really happens, many times, at many weddings—and not just for floral design, but in every specialty. We've seen it. If you want to take a chance, go ahead. But realize what might be at

stake.

Finally, you and your spouse-to-be should agree on the people you hire. If one of you—Bride or Groom—votes against a certain person then look elsewhere. No florist, photographer, DJ or caterer is so good that they are worth causing strife over. There will be plenty of important battles the selection of wedding vendors isn't really one of them.

Whoever you hire, they will be doing their best to do a good job for you. If things don't go perfectly, as happens once in awhile, it won't be because they aren't trying to do their best for you.

FINISHED PAGES 2-5

It's Your Day

Your Wedding Day

Your wedding day is probably the largest event you'll ever organize for yourself. It may also be the only one you ever get to do that has an almost *carte blanche* expense budget. Not that the sky's the limit, but weddings and receptions are the events reported by most families as the largest, most expensive gathering they've ever put together.

Aside from the expense, there is a question of what kind of day it will be — the style of the day. No matter how you frame it, you'll still have some standard expenses. The major ones described in this publication and a few more that you might decide to add. They'll all fit into their standard slots during the day. Though styles of wedding may change a bit, the caterer still caters, the photographer still photographs, and the music plays on.

Large, Medium, or Intimate?

The size of your wedding will usually be gauged by the num-

ber of guests. A "large" wedding is one with about 250 or more invited guests. A list of from 50 to about 250 is considered "medium," and below 50 guests it's an "intimate" or small wedding.

This is the first consideration. The classic wedding movie "Father of the Bride," with Steve Martin, comes to mind. Sometimes a guest list takes on a life of its own and grows beyond everyone's expectations. It gives you your first opportunity for give-and-take negotiation or Kabie-bar-the-door arguments!

Ultra-Formal to Casual

Once you've decided on the size of the wedding, the budget you have available can be used to help decide the level of formality. For "ultra-formal" picture tails and top hats for the men, and a long, formal train on the Bridal gown. All the Dads wear similar garb, and the Moms are dressed to the nines. The "formal" wedding means Tuxedos and a gown with a shorter train. "Semi-formal" might mean your groom and his guys wear suits, your

THE WEDDING PROFESSIONAL TRIO

MERCED'S Yosemite Floral
- Fresh Floral Arrangements
- Custom Silk Arrangements
- Decorations

Pat Linderos
722-7444
800-726-2837

3842 NORTH 'G' ST • MERCED
RALEY'S SHOPPING CENTER

Starfish Catering & Events
Breakfast • Luncheons • Banquets
Gorgeous Buffets / Sit Downs
Weddings are our specialty!
Outdoor Garden Weddings & Event Package

- Caterer & Liquor Liability
- Full Bar Service
- Fonts
- Round Tables & Chairs
- China & Linen

(209) 358-6030
Pat & Tralen Peterson

BEAR CREEK Travel
We make Honeymoon Dreams come true!

Hawaii, Mexico, Disney & Cruise — Specialists —
Ask About Our Honeymoon Registry

209-385-6377
2853 G Street, Merced

Bridal gown has a short or no train, and the Dads wear suits.

Beyond the levels of "formal" weddings, there are the "casual" weddings — so-called only for lack of a better term. Suits replace tuxedos and one-length or cocktail-length Bridal gown might be selected. Some of the most fun we've ever had and seen guests having as happened at these non-formal events. People are in their own clothes, they're more relaxed, and the focus is on people, not procedures.

Theme Weddings

Want to have some real fun? Cowboys? Victorian Ladies and Gentlemen? Knights and Damsels? Galactic Invaders? Prospectors? How about holidays, such as Christmas or Valentines that watch the price of gowns? Once you've decided on a theme, the planning of the wedding and reception (which can both use the same theme) takes on an entirely different feeling. Suddenly when you get into a planning session, the question isn't "Now, what are we supposed to do at *this* point?" It's more often "Why don't we do *this!*" Imagination takes over, where before there was tradition and procedure. Ideas begin to flow. Laughter is heard in the land once again.

If everyone is in agreement about having a theme wedding day it can be as lavish or earthy as you wish. For instance, a French Revolution-era theme could either be Marie Antoinette's court, or the class of Canton, the revolutionary. An historical British theme could either be King Arthur and Guinevere, or just one of the Knights. On a futuristic note, how about Queen Amidala (Padme) and Anakin Skywalker tying the knot on a balcony overlooking a beautiful lake? The musicians would certainly enjoy playing some John Williams themes. You could do it at a golf course or country club, overlooking a water-trap at sunset.

Your theme can be less involved than these. With only minor costumes you can do Gilligan's Island on any beach, then write a reception meal in the sand at a nearby beach-front hotel.

Once you've decided to have a theme wedding, the only restriction is your imagination!

Carrying Through With Your Style

Whether you have a good of American wedding (with its standard combination of historical traditions from our Scottish, English, Irish, German and other ancestries), or you decide to recreate something from Star Trek, your invitations, food and drink, music, and everything else can follow in that style.

How This Publication Is Organized

Regarding your search for wedding day services, you might want to consider interviewing for them in a certain order. Consider videography. The majority of weddings have a professional videographer. And just all videographers' results are the same.

Here's the rub: A specific videographer's work, that you might like, can't be done by anyone else. It's a personal set of skills, talent and technical expertise. The point is, if you want this person, you need to hire him or her for your wedding before anyone else!

So this publication is organized around the principle: First Things First! Don't miss the major services you want because you're consumed with minor things. First, you should nail down the most limited services: e.g. locations, photography, videography, catering, music. Don't miss the Reception hall you like because you were listening to CDs to choose the tunes for your first ray and dance!

If you go through the Contents and then our articles, you'll see that the organization is based on booking those services and products first that might not be there later.

The ideal place for your perfect wedding!
Situated on the beautiful campus of the University of the Pacific
- Rose lined walks & mature trees
- Exquisite stained glass
- Dark wood tones
- Seating for 300
- Ceremony Coordinator

Join us February 18, 2003, for Weddings 101
A free, one evening course on the ins and outs of planning your perfect wedding

Morris Chapel
(209) 946-2538

3601 Pacific Avenue, Stockton, CA 95211
http://www3.uop.edu/studentlife/religious_life/weddings.html

Choosing Professional Wedding Service Providers

Of all the states of decisions you'll make in preparation for your wedding day, the several that are the most important concern the professionals you will hire for your wedding and reception. It is their services and quality that will determine the success of your day.

You can plan, and plan, and plan. But the carrying out of the plan depends on how well you hire pros whose services match your plan, and how good they are at their services.

So, it's a three step process.

1) Decide exactly what you want.
2) Find some professionals who can deliver it.
3) Hire the best ones.

If you get the impression that the success of the wedding day is up to you, from beginning to end, you're right. This is a pragmatic way of looking at things, and it works.

For example, if you decide you want a Polish Theme Wedding, and you hire Mariachis and ask them to

play Polkas... well, you get the point. It's a ridiculous example, but the same kind of mismatch can happen. For example, if you want a formal photographic coverage of the wedding, but you hire a photographer who calls himself a photojournalist stylist just because he's a less expensive. He will disappoint you—not necessarily because he isn't good, but because he is trying to work outside of his area of specialization. The same goes for the other services in your wedding. You want French food? Don't hire Good OI' Boys Barbecues as your caterer.

Part of making the right decision also revolves around talking to the people or person who will actually provide services for your wedding. If you hire a DJ for your reception, you should be sure to talk to the person who will be loading the CDs. This applies to all of your services. Videography, photography, ceremony musicians, officiant, etc. It just makes sense.

When you've found the people you think will be able to provide the services you want, ask for their contract. A lot depends on their reliability as a business: a contract that specifies who, when, what, where, and for how much will help to guarantee their attention to details. Don't get the impression you have to "protect yourself" from anyone. On the contrary, it's just a good business practice on the part of any business to have a ser-

vice contract. It's a form of communication, not a sword of discipline.

What about asking professionals for references? It's a good idea, but remember: you'll get the list of clients whose weddings or receptions went perfectly, the others won't be included. You'll at least have the chance to find out what kind of job the vendor can do when things go right.

In many cases, you should be talking to the person who will actually provide your services, if you aren't, there is no point in talking. Of course this doesn't apply to the rental of equipment, banquet rooms, or your ceremony location. It might not apply to other services such as floral design or balloon art, but there are a few to which it does strongly apply. They are videography, photography disc jockey services, any provider of live music, your officiant, and your coordinator/consultant. Many of these wedding services fare extra people to meet the demand, you will want to talk to the person who will be assigned to serve you before you commit to a particular company.

One other important consideration is this: Do you like the person and feel good about working with her on your wedding day? Given the underlying stress of the day and how it can strain even good relationships, it's important that you consider the personality of

everyone you'll work with. Your videographer will be there constantly, but might not be directing you very much. However, your photographer, especially if he or she is of the "traditional-formal" style, will be directing you quite a bit. Your coordinator will be with you from start to finish. If you like your officiant, you will have a better memory of the ceremony

even though he or she will be with you only a part of the time. When these people give direction and instruction—as they must in order to do their job for you—you will want not to be irritated by it!

But wait: *Do you really need to hire professionals for your wedding?* If you are working to budget for them, the answer has to be yes. There are several good reasons for this not the least of which is that you'll get what you expect or want to have them. You've just been there but beyond that can consider your wedding day. It's a day you've dreamed of and planned for. It's a day you want to be the best it can be. Do you want to risk a friendship over it? Imagine that your best friend says she will do your flowers? Yes. Maybe she's a floral design

major at a local trade school, or maybe she's really good with flowers. She does her best, but on your wedding day your flowers are nothing like you would have ordered and received from a pro. What do you do? Do you have the assertiveness to tell her that she let you down? Can your friendship survive if it you do? Will you still feel the same way about her if this happens, whether you say anything or not? This situation really happens, many times, in many weddings—and not just in floral design but in every specialty. We've seen it. If you want to take a chance, go ahead. But realize what might be at

stake.

Finally, you and your spouse-to-be should agree on the people you hire. If one of you—Bride or Groom—votes against a certain person, then look elsewhere. No florist, photographer, DJ or caterer is so good that they are worth causing strife over. There will be plenty of important battles, the selection of wedding vendors isn't really one of them.

Whoever you hire, they will be doing their best to do a good job for you. If things don't go perfectly as happens once in awhile, it won't be because they aren't trying to do their best for you.

LICENSED TO MARRY

In California, the standard Marriage License is good for 90 days and can be used anywhere in the State. No blood test is required, but you must both be present to apply. Each of you must present two forms of ID. You may use your Birth Certificate instead of a second photo I.D.

California also issues a "confidential" marriage license, which keeps your information from becoming public record. To apply for it, you must be living together as husband and wife. Other than this, the same regulations apply.

If either of you have become divorced within the previous 12 months, bring your divorce decree with you. If the divorce decree was issued more than 12 months previously, you will need to know the exact date of the dissolution.

If you are under the age of 18 or are not an American citizen, other requirements apply.

For more information, call your **County Clerk-Recorder's** office. (In the phone book under "County Government Offices," also may be listed under **Marriage Licenses** in the same section.)

TREASURES

Merced & Co.

For the two of you ...

Everything You'll Need For the wedding and reception You've dreamed of.

Ideal for inside or outside Wedding and Parties
- Gazebo
- Church
- Catering
- Courtyard
- 160 Beautifully Appointed Rooms

Stay at our Spanish style Mission with outdoor heated pool and spa, full-service restaurant and lounge, and elegant banquet, meeting and conference facilities.

Resort style atmosphere located on over 15 acres

RAMADA INN MISSION de ORO
(209) 826-4444
(800) 546-5697
fax (209) 826-8071

13070 South Hwy 33 at I-5, Santa Nella, CA 95322

OLE for Photos and Graphics

What "OLE," or "Open Linking and Embedding," means is that a "link" is placed in your publication to the high-resolution graphic or photo that will be used for printing when it's needed; the high-res graphic is not made a part of the publication file while you are working on it. All you see on the computer screen is the low-res, screen-resolution version of it—a place-holder.

The high-res version, which will be used for printing, can be held in a separate (or the same) folder or directory. A link to it is embedded in your publication file. This process is completely invisible to you, done automatically by the program. It allows the working publication file to stay smaller and faster to work with. (It also saves disk space, because the original high-res graphic file does not have to be duplicated in your publication file.)

When the publication is printed (or saved as a press-quality PDF), the link to the high-resolution photo or graphic is activated, and the computer substitutes the high-res version for the low-res version you see on screen. It is all automatic.

What you *must* do, however, is *be sure* the link in your publication file accurately points to the actual location of the photo or graphic. (If it doesn't find it, the low-res, jaggy, screen-resolution version will automatically be substituted: You won't like it.) This is why it is a good idea to always create in advance a specific folder on your hard drive to hold the photos and graphics files. You will keep all of the high-res versions there, and the publication file will always know to look for them there. (Note: If you change the location or name of this folder, even by one space or underscore, you will break the link. Once you've established it, don't change it.) See the diagram of the "New Edition Folder" on page 44. If you move the high-resolution version out of the linked folder after you've placed it in the publication, you will get error messages.

Page 121: Place Your Photographs

Having processed and saved your photos for this page in the "Photos_Being_Used" folder, you can now place them into the boxes you've provided.

The numbering of photos, as mentioned before, will assist with your organization. For example, the photos on page 2 would be named "02a_(photographer/business name).tif" and "02b_(photographer/business name).tif."

Page 122: Final Placement of Photos and Advertisements

In the pages shown on page 122, the layouts are completed, shown just as they were printed in the 2004 San Joaquin Valley edition that year. All advertisements, additional text boxes, photos, etc., are in place. (Download the complete PDF of that edition from our site: **www.WriteAMagazine.com**.)

After you know exactly where your photos will go on the page, and what you want to do with them, you can manipulate their size in any way you want. Bleed them off one edge, two edges, three edges, four. Feather them into the text. Gray them out and put text over them, using them as a background. Convert them to stark graphics, add textures, etc. You are the designer; you may use all the design tools at your disposal. (If you only change their size or crop them, you can do it in your page layout program. However, if you change their tonality—feathering or graduating an edge to white, lightening the shadows so you can put type over the photo, etc., you should do it in your graphics program.)

Credit For Contributing Photographers and Advertisers

Accreditation for photos is something I take quite seriously. During one ten-year period of my life, I was a wedding photographer in California. Now, in the wedding planning magazines I publish, I put a copyright notice and credit line on every single photo, right under or beside it, in a readable type size. I also give a reference to the page the advertiser's ad is on. (Of course, I only allow advertisers to submit photos for the magazines.)

At times, this leads to some unreasonable requests and demands on the part of advertisers. At the beginning of this business, I set up a "policy" for placement of advertisers' photos. First of all, I will use at least one photo from anyone who sends photos, no matter how bad it is or how much work I have to do to make it look good. Secondly, I do my best to *not* put a contributed photo on the same page as the advertiser's ad. There's a simple reason for this that I have established, and since I'm the publisher (as you will be) this established rule is "law." The reason is twofold: I primarily feel that putting the photo on the same page as the ad gives the advertiser an apparent advantage, but doesn't really give any marketing assistance, since the reader will see the ad on the same page in any case. I also feel, though, that putting the photo(s) on other pages will lead the reader to seek the advertiser's ad, out of curiosity if nothing else. In effect, it gives the advertiser an additional mention in the magazine. That's my story, and I'm stickin' to it.

Once in awhile, though, my sales reps "give in" and "promise" an advertiser that the picture they supplied will be on the same page. In some cases, I give in; in others, I don't, and I take the heat from both of them.

A Note About Backups and Disasters

If you don't back it up, you will lose it. It might not happen for years, but when it does, you will rejoice if you've made backups. You'll feel very sick if you haven't.

Making a backup of the publication file is a simple, easy matter. There are certainly better backup schemes, but this one is better than most folks actually use.

Every time you close your publication file or go for lunch, dinner, or to stop for the day, make a duplicate of your publication file. That's all.

You may have lost data in the past because a file has become corrupted. After all, who hasn't? If you make a duplicate every time you quit, you'll never lose much. And, the failure of your hard drive, though it will happen eventually and probably destroy everything you have on it, is much less a threat than the corruption of your publication file.

On the drive of my computer, as I write this, is the duplicate file I made two hours ago, just before I stopped to have lunch. In addition to this procedure, I also save my current file with a keystroke at least every ten minutes.

And, in addition to all of that, I use the Mac's automatic full backup process, called "Time Machine," about every two days.

Why am I so attentive to it? Because I once experienced a head-crash on a hard drive that had with an entire magazine on it. It wasn't backed up. It took three weeks just to get back to the point where I lost everything. Some important items were never recovered.

THE HOME STRETCH

Create the Advertiser Index

On your sales contracts, even though you ask for the "Exact Business Name," you won't get it. You will get the name of the business as your sales rep knows it. By waiting until your ad is in place, you can look through the publication file on screen (or read through the printed copy you will use for proofing) and simply make a list from the ads.

I use a spreadsheet program to do it. Any spreadsheet program will do — even the free Google version online. I simply go through the magazine page by page, logging all of the placed ads on page 2, then page 3, then page 4, etc., to the end of the magazine, making an entry for the business name, the page, and the specialty heading as I go. It looks like this:

Business Name	Page	Specialty title
Morris Chapel	3	Event Location
Maciel's Jewelry	4	Jewelry

... and so forth, through the entire magazine. I do it this way because only the ad itself always shows the correct business name, and also just to be sure to get the page numbers right. Barring typographical errors, it works pretty well.

After typing it into the spreadsheet program, I alphabetize the entries by their specialty headings, so I'll have all of the Event Locations together, Caterers together, Photographers together, etc. Then, within each specialty, I highlight and sort alphabetically the business names and their page numbers. Next, I insert an empty row above the business names and type in the Specialty Title for each set of businesses in that specialty. Finally, I erase the column with all the original specialty labels, so I'm left with just the Business Names and their Page Numbers, with each group headed by its Specialty Title.

Copy it into the page layout program, format the type so the index is easy to use, insert the tabs to the page numbers, proofread it, and it's done. It takes about two hours. See an example on the next page; to this one, I added the website URL for each business.

Contents

Lay it out however you want. On the Contents page, I also include these: 1) A writeup on the cover photographer. The extra writeup helps keep 'em happy. 2) Publication info: Who to call for advertising, the publisher of the magazine, etc.

Proofread and Polish It, Then Have It Proofread Again

Proofreading consists of more than just "reading." It's especially risky for the writer of the work to proofread it. A writer reading his or her own words will read what was intended to be written—not always what is actually on the page. It's best if a different mind and set of eyes proofreads the work *after* the writer's read-through and polish job.

The Hard Part Is Done! Congratulations!

You've done it: You've produced a magazine! Now, all you need to do is create your covers, and send it to the printer. Those parts are actually a lot of fun.

Advertiser Index and Website Directory

Category & Name	Website or E-mail	Category & Name	Website or Email

Chapter 21

Everyone hated the 1996 cover of the San Luis Obispo edition, so I went super-simple for the 1997 cover. I've stayed simple since then.

YOUR COVERS

"You don't get a second chance to make a first impression."

This old saying definitely applies to magazine covers, as does, "You can't judge a book by its cover." (But we do, don't we?)

Imagine that you're an engaged woman, browsing in a stationery store that sells wedding invitations from those huge catalogs. You see a magazine across the room, in a little rack on a counter. On the front, in big letters, is the word, "Wedding." Other words are there, too, but you don't see them. You see the face of a Bride, or a Bride and Groom. You walk toward the magazine. As you approach, you also see the word "Free," or "Complimentary Copy," in the right corner where the price usually is.

You pick up the magazine and take it home, amazed that such a nice publication costs you nothing.

Another scenario: Maybe you're a newcomer to "Wherever City," anxious to find information on some good gyms, so you can stay in shape. You walk into a sporting goods shop, and on the way in, you notice that a little magazine rack sits on the counter. It shows someone in a spinning class and a guy working on a big Cybex leg press machine on the cover, and its title is "In Training! ... Wherever City." Your search has ended.

Or maybe you want to buy a home. Beside the real estate listing magazines at the supermarket entrance, in the same rack, is a little magazine with a color cover of a partially built two-story home. Its title is, "Your New Home In Wherever City."

You pick up both of them. They'll clearly be useful to you before and after you buy your home.

You name it, and the subject can be nicely covered in a local magazine. When people look at the cover, they don't examine it too closely, except to be sure it is about the subject of their interest and that it looks like it's worth carrying to the car and keeping. (Later, they might examine the cover and see small technical faults, but they won't reject it because of them.)

It's my feeling that there's no reason to break the probably-unwritten cover illustration rules followed by most national magazines. If it's a women's magazine, it always has a beautiful woman on the cover, either just a face shot or, at most, a three-quarter-length photo. The eyes of the cover model are invariably looking right at you.

It's much the same with the wedding magazines on the rack. You usually see a photo that is, without doubt, a beautiful, happy bride, looking at you.

On the national magazines about homes, building, decorating, etc., you see photos of homes, building projects or decorating projects.

On Outdoors magazines, you see a kayaker at the edge of a raging river in a beautiful setting, or a hiker with a towering mountain peak in the background.

Don't Try To Get Artsy

In the same way that an ad's only job is to identify a business's product or service, to display the phone and address, and generate a call or visit, the magazine cover's only job is to attract the eye and grasping hand of the potential reader. Once that's been done, and the word "free" is noticed, it's a sure bet that the person will pick up the magazine and take it home.

After they take it home, your content must keep it in their hands—but that isn't the job of the cover. The cover has done what it should.

Simple and Attractive

The recipe (except for the 1996 cover, when I got carried away) was and is:

1) A photo of a Bride or Bride and Groom, at least as close as waist-up, with the Bride's flowers prominent in the photo (because florists are important advertisers).

2) The title, large and prominent.

3) The edition name and the word FREE at the very top.

4) At the bottom, the photographer's credit, and my slogan, "The Only Complete Guide for the (CITY) Bride."

On some covers, I've used short "teaser" copy. However, the rule now is to include only the items listed above. It makes for a simple, inviting cover, with the title and the photograph the most prominent elements of the design.

Scanning Not Needed

These days, your selections for cover shots will all be digital. When you open them in Photoshop, they will be huge — a JPG about 50 inches wide, at 72 dpi, because pro photographers use high-megapixel cameras (12 to 21Mp per shot), and they are saved as a 72 dpi JPG, or RAW. Don't be put off by this.

The first thing you should do is crop them approximately the way you will want them, and then, in the "Image>Image Size" dialog box, change the resolution to 300 dpi at about 12 inches wide. Leave enough room so you can do further cropping or composing of the photo.

Remove blemishes, lighten, darken, sharpen, etc.

After all of those procedures are done, you can add your title and additional text lines. As mentioned above, I usually put the title, the publication's location and year, and the word "free." I also add a small "© John Jones Photography" at the bottom of the cover.

But, If You Scan?

If you are scanning photos for your cover, you will want a glossy 8x10. Scan at 600 ppi, in RGB (not CMYK) color. This will create a data file in your graphics program that is over 100 Mb in size. The first thing you'll want to do, if it's an 8x10 original, is increase its size so that the area you'll actually use for the cover will be at least 11 1/4 inches high by 8 3/4 inches high, if your trim size is the same as a letter-size sheet (which I recommend). Why these dimensions? You will want your cover to "bleed," that is, to go right off the edges of the trimmed cover paper. You'll have to allow a "bleed area" for this to happen, and with most printers, the "bleed area" is 1/8 inch. (This allows for paper movement on press.) You'll also need to color-correct it.

It can get complicated. Best thing to do is work from high resolution digital files. Only scan if you cannot avoid it.

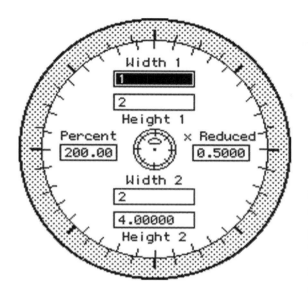

Chapter 22

SEND IT TO THE PRINTER

Until 1996, I was like most other little (and some big) publishers. I would print the individual pages of the magazine, all text in place. I had paid a bunch of money for a 1000-line-per-inch laser printer in 1992, and used specially coated paper, to get the sharpest, finest type I could from it.

I would print out all of the type, with boxes for the photos, each one numbered.

Then, I would put together all the photos I had selected, use my computer-based circular "photo reduction calculator" (shown above, like a circular slide rule), and calculate the reduction percentage and cropping for the printer. Then, I'd collect all the camera-ready ads I couldn't scan or paste in, number them carefully, and package them. I'd do the same with lithographic negatives sent to me by advertisers.

Finally, I'd make sure it was all there, package it in a Federal Express box, and send it off. It took me almost four weeks to do the paste-up and layout job. If it was all labeled correctly, the printer would return to me in about two weeks a "blueline" proof, showing everything in position. This was usually what happened. There were errors to fix, of course, and that was the function of the blueline proof.

A few years later, with the infrequent exceptions of litho negatives for ads and color separations for full color ads, I was sending everything on a CD or DVD, depending on the size of the project. Everything quickly became digital, and it was so easy as compared to the old way of doing it, that I could hardly believe it.

And now? Incredible how easy it is to prepare a publication for the printer, thanks to the ubiquitous Adobe Acrobat and Adobe's wonderful PDF file structure.

You see, it is now so easy because all I have to do is print a PDF, using the X-1a file definition (which is built into the leading page layout programs like InDesign and QuarkXpress).

The quickness of transmitting files to the printer (as PDFs online, uploaded to the printer's computer), and the ease with which you can make changes and alterations, might lead you to be less than diligent in proofreading and checking. But the ease of it all can lull you into making costly mistakes. It seems so easy and quick to do everything, that you might forget about the fees for making a single change on any single page: It costs $56 per page change with the printer I use. It doesn't take many of these to teach us the wisdom of careful proofreading.

It costs about $70 for me to print a complete 104-page full-color PDF at the local CopyIt shop. I not only get the opportunity to see the publication's color, but I also can see, full-size and full-resolution, the quality of everything on every page. If I'm careful in proofreading, I will not only avoid the costs of making changes or alterations (called AA's, or "Author's Alterations), but I will also avoid delays in production. I consider it money well spent. And, it's nice to see it in full color at this point.

The Proofs You Receive

Blue Line: A "BlueLine" proof is a complete copy of the magazine, made from the page negatives, bound as the final publication will be, but all imaged on photographic "blue-print" type paper. (And, sometimes, the imaging is in a light brown on the "blueline." Go figure.)

These days, you might not receive a blueline, but instead a bound copy printed on a high-resolution imagesetter, bound the way your finished product will be bound. The advance of technology has provided a better proofing product for us.

You might also receive plate prints — full-size, full-color 4- or 8-up sheets that show the pages as they will be on the printing plates. The printer I use, American Web in Denver, sends both types of proofs. It's a kick to see the beautiful color press pages, and it provides a chance to be sure all the important elements of your pages are inside the trim and bleed lines. Last year, I found a major title on a two-page color ad spread that the trim would have cut off. My error in placement cost me $56 to fix, since it was an AA ("Author's Alteration") but if I hadn't been able to fix it, the advertiser would have wanted and deserved more as a settlement for my bad handling of the ad.

If you see a problem in the proofs, and you don't direct the printer to fix it, the printer *will not* fix it. Printers do not make changes unless you direct them to do so. The blueline is the last step at which you can make a correction before the job is put on press, and the entire job committed to many hundreds of thousands of sheets of expensive paper, for a full year's distribution.

It literally pays to proof carefully, then, *before* you send the job to the printer, because changes made at the blueline stage are expensive. Sometimes, you don't catch an error until you see the blueline, and you feel like an idiot for not seeing it previously—but this should not happen for lack of trying beforehand. Look for big errors, too—not just details. Headlines have a funny way of being misspelled and not caught, for example.

When *your* error is caught and corrected on a blueline, you will be charged for an Author's Alteration. When you catch a *printer's* error on the blueline, you will not be charged for the correction. Sometimes, it is a good idea to make a note or a photocopy of the changes and corrections you make; printers sometimes call a correction an AA, when it shouldn't be. (Your final, itemized invoice from the printer will have a line that reads "Three AA's at $56.00 ..... $168.00," or something like that. If you made only two alterations, you don't want to pay for their correction of their error.)

Shipping & Receiving

Many printers will arrange this for you and add it to the final invoice. This is easiest and usually the most cost effective.

You might need to pay sales tax if you are shipping out of state. Laws vary, so check on it.

A Final Word On Responsibility

Printers print what you send them. If you make a mistake in someone's ad, or if you err in a title, or if you leave a telephone number out of an ad and don't notice it on the blueline proof, you have to live with it. The printer will give you nothing back for it; it is your responsibility, and your responsibility only, to make sure your print job is correct. The printer is not obligated to, and normally will not, proofread anything for you. If they notice something out of the ordinary, they *might* note it for you, but it's not their responsibility to do so. And, even if they notice a mistake and bring it to your attention, if you don't tell them to fix it—or simply write "stet" (Latin: don't change it) on the notation—they will not change it.

This will be made clear in the printer's agreement and contracts. What you send is what they will print—and ignorance on your part is no excuse.

Having said that, I must also say this: Printers always have a "make-good" policy, whereby they will take care of their mistakes. One time, the printer I used for eleven years committed a binding error on 2,500 magazines out of a printing of 9,000. They went back on press with the entire job and immediately shipped an additional 2,500 copies, without a whimper. It took them only ten days to get the replacements to my sales rep. This is why I used the same printer for eleven years. (Sundance Press, in Tucson, Arizona. You simply can't find a more helpful printing company. Anywhere.)

Chapter 23

DISTRIBUTING THE MAGAZINE

Your potential readers, being a targeted market, can be found in specific places—the businesses of your advertisers. This is an important point to remember, because the commercial "magazine stands" are probably closed to you as a "small magazine publisher." Because most people don't know about the "magazine stand" distribution system, I'll explain it. First, though, let me mention generally how you *can* distribute.

So, How Are These Magazines Distributed?

Let's say you have 10,000 magazines to distribute throughout the year, and 50 advertisers. If you divided the copies equally, each sponsor would receive 200. But, that would not be a good idea.

Some advertisers have higher volume than others. Some are seen at an earlier stage in a project. If you are decorating a house, for example, who do you see first? An interior decorator would be my guess. Other high-on-the-list services would be carpet outlets, paint stores, furniture showrooms, and window-covering stores. If yard installation and care is part of your subject, you would also want to distribute at stores where they design and install sprinkler systems, etc. The smaller outlets, such as the window tint company mentioned elsewhere, would not need as many copies. Nor would very small businesses without retail locations.

Your strategy would be to place the bulk of your magazines at the locations of advertisers who have the highest customer traffic volume. You would want to distribute about half of your magazines at the beginning of the most active season for your subject, and replenish as necessary throughout the publication year.

For my wedding magazines, the major distribution points are these: Bridal salons, coordinators and consultants, photographers, florists, reception locations, and jewelry stores. Others, in the "second tier," are musicians and DJ's, independent officiants, caterers, limousine and carriage companies, dieting systems, travel agents, etc.

The idea, if it's not obvious, is to place the most copies at locations every customer visits, and fewer copies at those locations that not every customer uses. For weddings, the major spots are reception hall, photographer, florist, wedding gown from a bridal salon, and rings. For home decorating, the interior decorator comes to mind as a top choice, along with the carpeting, etc. For your subject, you will need to discover these kinds of things.

You will discover quickly who is distributing and who is not. One month after your first distribution, simply contact everyone and ask how many copies they still have. Simple math will reveal your answers. (When you get to the end of the year, and your supply grows short, you will want to retrieve copies from some locations and place them at others, where you know they will be given away.)

Putting The Magazine Online

You will have a website to support your magazine. The site I use can be seen here: www.**WeddingAndPartyMag.com**. How you organize your site is an individual decision, but the question will come up: Should you put the entire magazine online for people to download? My answer to this is: *Yes!* I also maintain a separate website for rates, specs, etc. (**www.SLORates.com**)

The reason I put it online is so that the advertisers can know that their ad is available online, in place in the magazine pages. Their ads are visible in the website itself, as sidebars and as pop-up links, but they want to know that the reader of the PDF downloaded will see their ad in addition to their competitors' ads.

The Unavailable Commercial Distribution Chain:
How It Works and Why You Don't Want To Use It

1) Regional Distributors: The companies who maintain magazine stands in most grocery stores and news stands are regional distributors. These businesses receive bundles of magazines by truck from larger distributors, and they then place them on the shelves of local stores. Distributors normally serve a large region. You may have seen them working as you shop at times, with shopping carts full of bundles of magazines, taking old issues and replacing them with new ones.

These distributors must approve of and agree to distribute your magazines, and you must agree to pay them by their terms. (More on payments later.)

2) Chain Stores: If you want to distribute your magazines at an Albertson's Food Store, you must show the magazine and get advance approval from the Albertson's division office for your region. Same with Safeway, Kroger, and every other chain.

After that, you must usually get additional approval from the district manager, and sometimes even the individual store managers.

After you get these approvals, you must agree to pay these stores according to their standard terms. (More on payments later.)

3) Bookstores: Barnes & Noble, Border's Books, and their subsidiaries, each have their own separate magazine distribution systems, within which you must work and from whom you must receive approvals. And, you must pay these folks, too. (Yep, you guessed it. More on payments later.)

4) Independent Magazine Outlets: Though they are few and far between, you can probably talk the owners of these shops into carrying your magazine on their shelves. But, you still have to pay them.

5) Payment: Here it is. The distribution company charges from 25% to 30% of retail cover price per copy to handle every magazine title they maintain. The chain store charges the same thing. So, on average, figure that you must give up 50% of the cover price of each magazine sold on a magazine stand. For some magazines, as a way of *discouraging* distribution by small magazines, the rates are higher.

So you will give up 50% of your cover price. If your magazines carry a cover price of $4.00 apiece, you will give up $2.00 for each one sold. (I'm using round numbers for convenience. The real price would be more like $3.95.) You will receive your payments from the distribution company, normally, within about 90 to 180 days. You will receive payment, at the rate of 50% ($2.00 per copy sold, in our example), *only for the magazines sold.*

What happens with the unsold copies? The distributor rips off their covers and sends the body of the magazines to a paper recycler. You get nothing for them, and no return of them.

With the check that you will receive in about six months, you get a statement saying how many copies were sold, their price, the amount you get, and the number of copies not sold (destroyed). These statements are usually accurate.

Figure It Out And Avoid It!

Let's say you are providing twenty copies of your magazine at each location. Your cover price is $4.00. You sell half of these, for $4.00 apiece. You average sales of 10 copies per location, or $40.00 per location. You get a total of 50% of that amount per location.

The sale of ten of those magazines will generate for you a check, in about six months, for the grand total of (drum roll, please...): $20.00 (Twenty dollars), and a statement saying the other ten copies were destroyed. Have a nice day.

Now, your costs for the magazines, if they are similar to my costs, will be about $2.25

per magazine. So, twenty magazines will cost you $45., for which you get back $20 after waiting six months to receive the payment.

Hm-m-m-m. Let's add up your profits: Payment of $20.00 received in six months, for twenty magazines that cost you $45.00 to produce.

So, why do magazine distributors use this system? First, it's the only game in town. Second, the larger magazines charge much more for advertising than you will, and their advertising rates are based on distribution. Their distribution figures are based on how many magazines they send to the stores to be sold, minus returns. Since it takes about six or more months for the returns to be subtracted and net distribution figures to come out, the magazines are effectively able to charge on all the magazines they put on the stands, plus subscription copies mailed out. Their numbers are inflated, giving them higher ad rates, so the number of unsold copies at the stores doesn't hurt them at all.

As you can see above, it would hurt you, Mr. or Ms. Small Publisher, so much you would go broke. But don't worry about it, because the distributors won't handle your magazine anyway!

So, How **Do** You Distribute?

Your advertisers will do the distribution for you. Simple as that. Every customer they see is a potential customer not only for their specific service, but for the services of many of the other advertisers as well.

By each of them distributing your magazine, they saturate the targeted market you need to reach. It is an excellent system: It provides the customers with a "free" source of information they need, and it creates the "Fuller Brush" effect for the retailer. (A free gift creating a sense of gratitude and goodwill.)

How Many Copies To Distribute

Whether your magazine is an annual, semi-annual, or quarterly, you'll want to make sure it is distributed throughout the entire publication period. The way I have set up my own business, this is the responsibility of the sales reps and is part of their contract. It helps them in their sales, too, if they are in contact with the advertisers from time to time. Calling the advertisers every couple of months to see how their supplies of magazines are holding out is a perfect way to maintain contact and let them build a relationship.

It's also nice that you don't have to do it.

Chapter 24

Customer Service Counts

I Led Two Lives

I was a secret shopper for a major grocery store chain, which shall be nameless but whose initial (and logo) is "S." My little job was to spend about 30 to 50 minutes in each store I was assigned to "shop," and to mentally note certain things having to do with basic customer service. They ranged from asking people where something was (to see if they would take me to it), to looking like I was searching unsuccessfully (so that a clerk working in an aisle would ask if he or she could help me find something), asking for special favors, presenting a problem a clerk could solve, checking on bathroom cleanliness, and all kinds of other items. After my clandestine shopping spree ended, I filled out and mailed a detailed 4-page form, directly to "S" headquarters. The form graded the store on every single thing you could think of, and many you wouldn't ever have guessed at. The store managers were paid their year-end bonuses based on how well their store did all year long, having been "shopped" by a different "shopper" every week. That's why "S" stores got a head start on others in this area; now, the other big chains are wising up, and their customer service has improved. (Ironically, "S" dropped the program, and now their customer service is not good.)

The job was interesting in many ways, in part because it sensitized me to the difference between *good* Customer Service and *neutral* customer service. Customer service is the key to repeat customers. It doesn't matter if you are publishing an annual magazine or if you are the neighborhood liquor store. If you don't provide the service, products, care, or problem solving needed and expected by the modern customer, you won't get their business more than once. There's plenty of competition for them to go to.

The interesting thing is, *good* customer service isn't noticed as much as *bad* service! Think about it: You easily remember the last time you were frustrated by not being able to locate something you needed in a store, but couldn't find anyone to ask. But, do you remember the last time someone met you in aisle 4 and took you all the way to aisle 11 to find a jar of pickle relish? Probably not. We take customer service for granted. We remember it when it's absent because it makes us angry and creates a specific memory. We expect

How A Dumb Mistake Happened

Unposed moments say more about you than a "Say Cheese!" picture.

NICOLE BOUGHTON, PHOTOGRAPHER
805/528-2899 • WWW.STORYBOOKPICTURES.COM

Above is the ad I used; below is the new one that I should have used. DUH! How did I blow it? Simple: I mislabeled the new one! It cost me $650 to learn the lesson: Always rename the graphic file for an ad by the name of the business, not the person! Because of my error, the phone number was wrong: I refunded the full amount of the ad cost and gave the advertiser a free ad the next year. It calmed the advertiser down and kept her in the magazine for five more years.

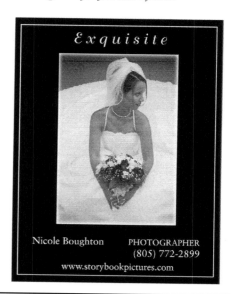

it to be "good."

When I make a major mistake on people's ads, like I did once with a photographer's ad, I do my best to take care of it. Here's a true recent story.

Nicole called me the day she got her copies of my latest magazine. She didn't sound angry, but she was upset because I had inadvertently printed her ad from the previous year's magazine! Oh, criminy, how could I have done such a stupid thing? (This was me talking to myself.) I had her new ad file, received via email, and it was completely different from the previous year's. Not only was the graphic content different, but the phone number was different from her current number!

I had severely damaged her business by making this mistake. She works from her home, by appointment only. She had dropped her Yellow Pages advertising because she gets 80% of her business from her ad in my magazine. Good grief. How would I ever be able to make this right?

Experience came to my aid. I had once used a service that some telephone companies called "remote call forwarding," which allows the customer to purchase the use of a phantom phone number—555-1234, for example—and have the telephone ring only at their "real" phone—555-4321. It's pretty slick, but it cost $17.50 per month. The catch, in this case, would be this: Was the telephone number that was in her incorrect ad (the one I printed) available, and did the telephone company offer the remote forwarding option?

I called the telephone number I had put in her ad. A recording told me it was disconnected or no longer in service. So, it was available. *Lucky!*

I called the phone company and confirmed that the number was available and that the remote service was also available. *Lucky again!*

I called Nicole and told her what I'd found out, how the remote service worked, and promised I would send her a check that same day for the full price of her advertisement ($530.00), *plus* the cost of the remote service for a full year (totalling $210.00). She was gracious, and said that she understood how mistakes happen, and said that if I would pay for just six months of the remote service, she would consider that more than generous. So, I mailed her, that day, a check for $650.00. It was a teeny bit more than we agreed, but I'm sure she appreciated it.

I talked with Nicole the other day, and she said her ad response is right up there with last year. *Whew! I am a lucky guy! I fell into the muck and came up smelling like a rose!* (But it cost me $650. to get my fragrance sweet again!)

Even though my contract with Nicole (on the Insertion Order) limited my liability to "...the amount of monies paid for the ad, even if due to the publisher's negligence,..." I felt bad about the error. Also, by going a bit farther than she expected, I made it a certainty that she would continue to trust my publication and pass that trust along to anyone who asks her about it. She stayed a customer for several years, until she moved away from the area.

All companies are great to work with when they've done a good job for you and you are happy about it. They prove their character, though, when something goes wrong. How are disputes handled? Is the customer fairly treated? Does the customer *feel* that he or she was fairly treated when a settlement became necessary?

Don't underestimate the importance of good, sincere customer service, even when your customer can't get the same service you offer anywhere else. If you let them down when they need your help, they will either dump you, or they will only grudgingly use your service or product. And, you can be certain they will tell others exactly how they feel—either way!

And, just to emphasize that point: The photographer whose ad I messed up was directly responsible for referring nine other wedding businesses to my magazine, and every one of them purchased ad space. They could have gone to my competitor, but they didn't. I'm convinced that it was the photographer's reference and story that brought them to me. So, in the end, I didn't lose, but gained, from the episode.

Chapter 25

Seven Little Rules For Success

1) Choose The Right Subject

This is probably obvious, but you'd be surprised at how many people will try to make a market support the subject they want to work with, when they should be finding a subject that is already supported by the market. It's also surprising how many people will choose something that simply *can't* be supported in a local market.

This book that you are reading is an example in itself. If I tried to publish it as a magazine, everything would be fine until I tried to sell ads in it. Then, I would hear the potential advertisers say, "Where's the local market?" I would have no answer, because there would not be enough of a local market to support this subject as a magazine, probably not even in New York City.

There are subjects that fit every market, like weddings, real estate, cars, babies, and a few others. Even in a small town, there is a collection of product and service businesses that surrounds these subjects. They can support a magazine that requires 100 advertisers.

There are also subjects that are inherent in cities or towns with certain properties. A college town can easily support a magazine devoted to newly-arrived students, because the entire town is the ad market. The idea would be to target the publication's information and ads toward college students who are looking for services they use all the time, like pizza places, garages, gas stations, clothing stores, liquor stores, grocery stores, pool parlors, and just about everything else.

But, if your subject isn't supported by the market, you can't make it so.

2) Stay Small

To some people, "small" might mean one magazine in one town. To others, "small" might mean three magazines in one town, each on different subjects published at different times during the year, and the same thing in two other towns.

The important thing is to find your niche. The reason why these kinds of magazines can prosper is precisely *because* they are small. They don't compete with national or even statewide publications. Their competition is the newspaper, which is terminally temporal, and the yellow paper phone book, which offers no information—just advertising.

Don't try to get too big, or you'll outgrow your market. If you want to expand, use the same basic text and publish in another city, or find another subject and publish in the same market.

The other aspect of staying small has to do with the subject of Chapter 5 (Where Will You Publish?). If you don't stay small, you might not survive.

And, finally, you don't want to add personnel: Staying small also means you want to keep it down to yourself, a salesperson, and the printer (and shipper from the printer to the sales rep).

3) You Don't Have To Do It All Yourself

The functions needed to publish these little magazines are a writer, graphic artist, sales person, and printer. In many cases, the writer can do the layout and design, with just a little bit of help.

Merely by following the formats we publish on our Layout & Design CD, a writer with little layout experience can produce a beautiful magazine. If you do it that way, the profit produced only has to be split two ways.

But, if you want to put together a 3-person team of writer, graphic artist and salesperson, there is still enough income to provide part-time income for everyone.

4) Show and Sell

The fact that you write and basically lay out the entire magazine before showing it to advertisers will give you a huge edge over other advertising media. When an advertiser can see exactly what he or she is investing in, and read the copy, then choose the best position available in relation to it, the sale is much more likely.

With other magazines, the newspaper, and even the yellow phone book, the advertiser must wait for it to come out before seeing where his ad will fall. With our business model, the position is already known in relation to the written copy. (However, because of layout requirements, an ad might have to be moved; this should be covered in your Insertion Order text.)

The only objections we've encountered were from people who just weren't sure the magazine would publish. These were people who had been ripped off in the past by individuals who promised a great publication, did a great sales job, and then took the deposit money and left town with it. However, with our sales presentation, complete preview edition, and a sales person who was or is in business locally (and might be known to the advertiser), this objection is easily overcome. For my wedding magazines, I insist on using people who are already involved in the local wedding market.

5) Quality is King

Don't publish something you can't be proud of. You *can* offer a cheaper price for ads, because if you use a "heatset newsprint" printing process, you can crank out 10,000 magazines for about $3,000. But, they have no feel of quality. They are like the weekly TV guide you used to get with your newspaper, or the weekend hardware store sale catalog. They are not kept around the house. Doctors and dentists will not allow them in their waiting rooms. (They work well for washing car windows.)

If you are inclined to do something with no quality, think about it from the advertiser's point of view. Would you want to associate your business with a cheap publication, or one that displays quality at a level that surprises and gratifies the reader when they find out it's free?

6) Keep the Sales Reps Happy

I negotiate commission rates with my sales reps. They earn about the same amount I do from each edition. I feel that I pay too much, sometimes, but then I have to remember: *My* income is in their hands!

It's a short rule. Keep them happy, and they'll earn money for you. If you neglect to convince them that you're doing the best you can for them, financially, their production will suffer. Your income will be lower.

7) Follow the Rules

Every business has a formula that works. This one is no different. If you pay attention to these details, you'll have a much greater chance of surviving and earning good profit from these little publications.

Undoubtedly, you'll discover additional rules for yourself. Use them and enjoy your business! Treat the other guy or gal well, just because that's the way you should treat him or her, and that's the way he or she should treat you. Otherwise stated, it's known as the Golden Rule: It pretty much takes care of all the other rules.

APPENDIX 1

STEP-BY-STEP OUTLINE OF THE ENTIRE PUBLISHING PROCESS

Below, is a complete outline, or flow chart, of the steps you will need to take and the order in which you'll take them. It's just a like cake recipe.

I. Decide on Subject

    A. Wide Local Market with business support

    B. Need for Information on part of Consumers

    C. Readers will soon make purchases within coverage of subject matter

    D. Subject on which readers won't need info soon again.

II. Find Your Market

    A. Publish where there are businesses

    B. Publish where there are readers

    C. Publish where there are no competing publications

III. Organize the Business by Edition

    A. Organize Computer with Folders per edition

    B. Organize physical files for Photos, Ads, Contracts, etc.

    C. Organize Workflow of forms, checks, etc.

IV. Get Printing Estimates

    A. Sheet fed or Web: Sheet fed best for under 10M

    B. Get Proforma estimates

    C. Use Estimates as basis of Costs

V. Hire An Independent Contractor Salesperson

    A. Must Fit The Subject Matter

    B. Not an Employee, but an Independent Contractor

    C. Self-Starter, Salesman (not an "order taker")

D. Should be local, experienced, and in subject business currently

E. Create and Execute the Contract Between You and Salesperson

VI. Computer Software/Hardware

A. Use Page Layout Program such as QuarkXPress or InDesign

B. Use Graphics Program—Photoshop best

C. Use Adobe Acrobat—Full version

D. Scanner—Nice to have even if rarely needed

E. Email capacity—up to 10mb to send and receive

F. Hardware - Mac or Windows: Mac preferred by most publishers

VII. Create Forms

A. Insertion Order (Ad Space Contract)

B. Rate Sheet: Establish Prices after next step

C. Graphics/Layout Guide

D. Ad Call/Phone Record Sheet

VIII. Create Your Preview Edition

A. Decide on Prices, Number of Ads

B. Page#/ABC-type Ad Grid (3A, 3B, 3C …)

C. Use Master Pages in Page Layout Program

D. Insert Greeked text (or actual text if written), graphics boxes

E. Print two copies as Comb-bound books at local xerography printer

IX. Hit the Road: Sales Begin (See also "X.D." below for order.)

A. Create Urgency with the Preview Edition (Buy best spot or competitor will)

B. Explain the market and the need for the publication

C. Sell the benefits, not the features

D. Compare this magazine with competing ad outlets

X. Meantime, Get the Finalized Writing Done

A. Make it Personal

B. Don't give too much information; just basic education in the subject

C. Let the advertisers be the experts

D. If possible, have writing done before sales period begins

XI. Process Sales

    A. Accept Insertion Order Forms w/checks

    B. Enter in Bookkeeping Program; Don't procrastinate!

    C. Deposit Checks in bank/File Forms in looseleaf notebook by page

    D. Mark Spaces SOLD in Preview Edition

    E. Note How Art is To Come; Set up Contact Date Tickler if not on time

XII. Payroll

    A. Pay Sales Rep partial commission when publication is assured

    B. Pay yourself partial payment when publication is assured

    C. Keep enough in reserve for printer

    D. After printing done, pay out balances to sales, self, printer

XIII. Finish Composing and Layout

    A. Place ads appropriately

    B. Place titles

    C. Place photos and graphics

    D. Place text

    E. Advertiser index, Contents, misc. copy

XIV. Proofread

    A. Detailed proofreading of complete printed PDF by at least two people

    B. Check phone numbers, addresses, names against Insertion Order

    C. Do not assume anything is correct! (Look for big errors, too)

XV. Create Your Covers

    A. Front

    B. Back and Inside

    C. Color correction?

    D. Service Bureau scan?

XVI. Collect Job and Export to PDFs using Printer's required file definition

    A. Print (Export) to digital PDF at "press quality"

    B. Make a complete backup of all files, **offline** on a hard drive or DVD(s)

XVII. Send It to Printer

    A. Upload Digital files or send on DVD

    B. Deposit check - according to printer's requirements

    C. Transmittal Letter with terms as you understand them, delivery address, etc.

XVIII. Get BlueLine and press-sheet Proofs

    A. Author's Alterations vs. Corrections

    B. Make only necessary changes because of expense

    C. Return to printer immediately

    D. Send additional deposit if required

XIX. Receive shipment of magazines & begin to distribute

    A. Retain copies for yourself

    B. Distribute with salesperson if local; meet your advertisers

    C. Distribute 1/3 to 1/2 at beginning, store others

    D. Call or drop in; see how supplies are moving; replenish as necessary

    E. Get info from advertisers about feelings toward mag, results, etc.

XX. Begin planning next year's edition or start work on a separate edition

These are the major steps plus some of the reminders I think are important. After twenty years of publishing multiple publications based on this system, it's likely that I've learned a lot about it, but "the unforeseen" is always there, waiting to reach around and bite you where you normally sit.

Take care of business, pay attention to detail, take nothing for granted, and you'll do just fine!

APPENDIX 2:
FORMS

These examples of these forms are in a "reduced" size so they can fit into the required page size.

At my website (**WriteAMagazine.com**), you can download the actual letter-size forms. They are not legal documents; if you choose to use them as legal documents, the risk is all your own. (Sorry.) I prepared them for my own use, and I am not a lawyer. As their author, I can neither guarantee their efficacy nor promise they will do exactly what you want.

They work for me, and have for years, but like I said, I am not a lawyer and I don't present them as examples of legally binding contracts; I accept no liability if they don't work for you.

Please accept this warning in the spirit it is offered (to protect myself **and** you). Have a lawyer look over any contractual forms you use in your business.

Wedding & Party AD CONTRACT CENTRAL COAST Edn: Pg# _____ Space_____

EXACT BUSINESS NAME_____

Contract Date: /_____/_____/_____/

Authorized Individual's FULL Name: _____ **Position:** _____

Mail Address: _____ **City & ZIP:** _____

Phone: _____ **EMAIL:** _____

AD SPACE PRICE (Black & White): ..$_____ **Website Address:** _____

– Full Payment Discount (if Applicable): .... $<_____>

+ COLOR PAGE ADDITION _____ $_____

+/– OTHER_____ $_____

= PRICE OF THIS AD: (Subtotal) .... $_____

– Payment With Contract : ....$<_____>

BALANCE DUE BEFORE PUBLICATION: $_____

MARK ad position on page by drawing a large "X"; if space is unavailable, ad will be moved to best available position.

A	E
B	F
C	G
D	H

←3.875" (3 7/8")→ ←2.375 (2 3/8")→

5.0" (5") 7.5 (7 1/2") 10.25" (10 1/4")

←8.0" (8") wide→

NOTE REGARDING AD

Ad Specs Online:
www.nichebooks.com/slospecs.html

ARTWORK DEADLINE: [_____]   **FULL PAYMENT-** [_____]

SOME CHARGES MAY BE ADDED AND BILLED AFTER THIS CONTRACT IS SIGNED ...such as ad graphics charges ($40 for a small ad to $100 for a full-page B&W ad; double rates if ad is in color), stripping charge ($25 per strip-in, to add a logo, change a phone number on an existing ad, add a website e-mail, replace a photo in ad) etc. Subject to all contractual terms below.

Payment made by: Check # _____ (OR) Credit Card Number: |__|__|__|__| |__|__|__|__| |__|__|__|__| |__|__|__|__|

Visa or MasterCard (card numbers beginning with 4 or 5 only.)

Cardholder Signature Required: SIGNATURE REQUIRED   Expiration Date: |__|__| / |__|__|—Amount $_____

We can re-charge your credit card when the balance is due. Card will not be charged until date written in "PAYMENT DEADLINE" box. Sign & date here to pre-authorize this: Signature: SIGNATURE REQUIRED   Date: REQUIRED

ART REQUIREMENTS:
Complete Art Requirements can be found on our Website: (www.nichebooks.com/slospecs.html). Please read and follow them. Call us with questions: 719-_____. IF YOU DON'T UNDERSTAND THE REQUIREMENTS, PLEASE HIRE A GRAPHIC ARTIST, see "Artists, Commercial" or "Graphic Design" in your Yellow Pages.

Your Ad Space **WIDTH** Is: _____ Inches. The **HEIGHT** is _____ Inches. Halftones/tints @ 300 dpi. Line art @ 600 dpi. Page Trim: 8.5" x 11.0". See RATE SHEET for full Ad Specs. Go to *www.nichebooks.com/slospecs.html* to see complete specs on internet.Full Page Ads may bleed all sides.
* * * *If sending mechanical art, CALL FIRST! * * * *

ADVERTISER HAS RECEIVED:	NOTES:
O Yellow Contract	_____
O Rates / Specs Sheet	_____
O Reception Site Form (if applicable)	_____
O Payment Due Date	_____
O Layout Guide	_____

PLEASE CHECK APPROPRIATE BLANKS:
New Advertiser? ____ Return Advertiser? ___ What Edition? (year)_____
Will Adv Provide: NEW Art?_____ Or Should We Use The PREVIOUS Art?_____
Will We Do Your Art?_____ Simple Scan of Business Card No Charge. All Other Graphics: See Rate Sheet. WE DO GRAPHICS; NOT "CREATIVE DESIGN". PLEASE SKETCH WHAT YOU WANT. (Too difficult to work long distance.) NO CHANGES AFTER ART DUE DATE. If sending mechanical art, CALL FIRST!

TERMS & CONDITIONS: THIS IS A LEGALLY BINDING CONTRACT. Advertiser named above has purchased this ad space subject to all terms outlined herein. The ad space purchased will be in the approximate position requested or the best available position; exact ad or page placement is not guaranteed. Publisher may refuse any ad for any reason. Publisher's maximum liability for errors or omissions in any ad is limited to the amount of monies previously paid by this Advertiser, even if such error or omission is due to Publisher's negligence. **DEADLINES:** It is the advertiser's sole responsibility to present ads and payment at Publisher's address on or before deadlines (written above). Publisher bears no legal or financial liability or responsibility for ad placement if any deadline missed by advertiser. **ARTWORK:** Failure to provide artwork constitutes a renege on this contract by advertiser. If "new artwork" is checked on this contract, but it does not arrive by deadline, the most recent other art from same advertiser will be used, without notification or "proof copy" to advertiser. If no artwork is received at Publisher's address on or before the due date written above, Publisher may, at its discretion, eliminate the ad, use a previous ad, or create a new ad. A graphics charge of up to $100 may be billed to the advertiser for ads thus created. **COLOR ADS:** ADDITIONAL CHARGE for color is based on additional production charges for color pages, not on coloration of the ad. **PAYMENT TERMS:** FULL PAYMENT is required prior to publication. DISCOUNT available ONLY FOR FULL PAYMENT WITH THIS SIGNED CONTRACT (or guarantee of payment via postdated check or valid credit card number & exp. date). Without guarantee, no discount is allowed. If payment is NOT RECEIVED ON OR BEFORE DEADLINE: Publisher may at its discretion remove the ad from magazine; Prepayments on hand will be retained at Publisher's discretion as liquidated damages for loss of revenue. If Advertiser has a balance owing from a previous edition or ad contract, full settlement of that debt is required and will be taken from any payments previously received; payment of any remaining balance for this contract's space usage is then due under the terms of this contract. If advertiser reneges on timely payment, publisher has the option of resorting to legal means to collect payment; advertiser understands that publisher may also sue for all costs of collection, including reasonable attorneys' fees, court costs, and travel costs if court appearance is required. **PROMISE TO PAY:** In addition to the herein described payment terms, this debt is also guaranteed as a personal debt by the advertiser/purchaser; the failure of the business does not release the business or its owner from this debt. **CANCELLATION/RENEGE:** This contract may only be cancelled by notice of cancellation in writing. If advertiser reneges on the contract by non-timely payment, by refusal to pay, or not providing artwork or art instructions prior to the artwork due date, the contract may be deemed cancelled on the missed due date: In such case, monies received become property of the Publisher, and advertiser's ad may not be published. **EFFECTIVENESS OF AD:** Advertiser is solely responsible for the ad's efficacy. Publisher's duty is to publish and distribute magazines; such publication and distribution completely fulfills publisher's duty under this contract. **COPYRIGHT IN MATERIALS SUBMITTED:** Advertiser warrants by submission of all materials that he/she/they/it is/are the legal owner(s) of Copyright in all photographs, artwork and textual material submitted for publication, whether said materials are submitted for use in paid ad space or editorial sections of the magazine. Advertiser absolutely indemnifies and will save harmless from any litigation Wedding & Party Magazine, Niche Publishing Company LLC, and all parties connected with ad sales and production of the publication, should copyright infringement or invasion of privacy be charged against the magazine for publishing materials submitted by advertiser and subsequently published with a good faith belief in the advertiser's ownership and right to publish same. **DISTRIBUTION** of the magazine is through selected advertisers and other appropriate outlets. Non-Advertising Businesses may not distribute magazines. All copies will be distributed FREE. Sale of magazines is expressly prohibited. **NO OTHER AGREEMENTS:** This contract contains the complete and only agreement between the Advertiser and the Publisher. **AUTHORIZED SIGNATURE:** As Advertiser's Authorized Agent, my signature below warrants that Advertiser accepts and agrees to honor all Terms & Conditions of this Contract, which I have read and which I completely understand.

SIGN & DATE   SIGN & DATE

ADVERTISER OR AUTHORIZED AGENT SIGNATURE/DATE   PUBLISHER'S REPRESENTATIVE SIGNATURE/DATE

Payments & Packages: WEDDING & PARTY MAGAZINE, Bill Cory,   EMAIL... [_____]

Form Distribution: White to Publisher With Deposit; Canary to Advertiser; Pink to Local Representative

Serving the Central Coast Wedding Industry Since 1990

AD SALES:

Wedding & Party
2009 California Central Coast Edition
http://www.weddingandpartymag.com

NOTE: PLEASE KEEP THIS SHEET FOR REFERENCE!

ALL PHOTOS, Ad Materials, Art, & Full Payment: **11-21-2008**

AD SPACE RATES: 2009 Edition
For Publication January, 2009

MasterCard VISA

Ad Sizes (Maximum Size Given)

	Space Rate	For Full Payment W/Contract Before Publication:
One-eighth page (3 7/8" wide by 2 3/8" deep): (Color, add $120)	$ 485*†	$ 455*†
One-Quarter-Page (3 7/8" wide by 5" deep): (Color, add $175)	$ 765*†	$ 725*†
Three-Eighths Page Vertical (3 7/8" wide by 7 1/2" deep): (Color, add $185)	$ 995*†	$ 955*†
One-Half Page Vertical (3 7/8" wide by 10 1/8" deep): (Color, add $200)	$ 1165*†	$ 1125*†
One-Half Page Horizontal (8" wide by 5" deep): (Color, add $200)	$ 1165*†	$ 1125*†

Full Page Ad Rates:

Inside Full Page (8.5" x 11.0"; may bleed all sides) (Color, add $245):	$ 1,585*†	$ 1,495*†
Inside Front/Back Cover (8.5" x 11.0"; may bleed all sides) (Color only):	$ 1,795*†	$ 1,745*†
Outside Back Cover (8.5" x 11.0"; may bleed all sides) (Color only):	$ 1,895*†	$ 1,845*†

*Plus Graphics Charge, if no art is provided by Advertiser OR if art is substantially below our quality standards. Fee provides logo & photo scanning, typography, proofs and one correction: RATES: Grayscale (B&W) 1/8 page size, $60; 1/4 or 3/8, $80; half or full page, $100. Color Graphics: Under 1/2 page, $70, 1/2 to full page, $100 plus rate upcharge above. One change to ad free; additional changes $25. each. This is a Graphics Service, not a Design Service; We will work only from your sketched idea. Clean LOGO art (Solid Black On White) needed.

†ADVERTISING AGENCIES: Rates above are NET. Agency Fee is to be added and charged to the advertiser.

DIGITAL ART SPECS: WWW.SLORATES.COM

COLOR ADS: Graphics charges may apply unless Advertiser provides: (1) Complete digital file as Photoshop TIF or PDF (.psd, or .tiff in RGB color). * * * * * *NOTE: FOR AD ART: WE NO LONGER ACCEPT LINE or SEPARATION NEGATIVES* * * * *

FREE EXTRA EXPOSURE

BRIDES LOOK AT THE PICTURES!

PHOTOS NEEDED:

FROM PHOTOGRAPHERS:

• A few photos of Bride and Bride & Groom Portraits; Some for COVER

• Bride & Parents

• Bride & Maids,

• Groom & Guys – serious and playful

• Misc candids Before, During, & After Ceremony

• Transportation

Reception Candids

• Buffet

• Toast, Cake, Cake Cutting

• Dancing

• Garter, Bouquet Toss, Catchers

• Misc Candids, serious and playful

• Candids of other participants & Pros

• Parents, Wedding Party Mbrs, Kids

FROM ALL ADVERTISERS:

• Your work or location, with or without Bride, Groom or Wedding Party Members.

• YOU working at weddings, but no "mugging" (standing beside your work and looking at the camera)

• No other restrictions; send 'em!

Sending PHOTOS on CD to ILLUSTRATE THE MAGAZINE: Please put all in one directory/folder. A thumbnail sheet is required w/photo and file name. Without it , photos may not be used.

If not possible, please send prints (8x10 maximum size per print; no minimum size)

Our magazines are illustrated with **local photographs** done by local advertisers. For all photos, the photographer/contributor retains Copyright. Credit and ad reference are given on every photo, such as "Courtesy of Cakeville Bakers, ad page 21," or "© Hi Quality Photos, ad page 38."

The Cover Photo is done by a local Professional Photographer; the front cover is not "for sale." We will use: Bride alone or Bride & Groom; her flowers mostly visible, full-length or closer. No payment is made to the photographer for the use of the photo; the publicity (with literally **every** Bride in the area seeing it) is worth much more than payment. All photographers who advertise are eligible. An unlimited model release allowing the photographer to use the image for advertising purposes is required; we will also provide our own model release which covers our use of the image for our purposes. **All photos sent are considered for cover; no need to mark or separate your choices.**

Inside the magazine, we use photos sent by all types of advertisers — not just photographers. (We'll try to use at least one of your photos, unless they are inappropriate or of no illustrative value.) This is a "photojournalistic" magazine, and as such, want photos other than "just pretty pictures of a Bride and Groom." We prefer a wide range of photographs. (See list at left.) When in doubt, send it!

All photos are returned. Color or Black & White, Max Size 8x10; no minimum size. Low-res digital photos will not be used. Framed photos will not be used or returned without prepaid postage.

QUESTIONS: Please telephone Joe [   ] (805-[   ]), or:
Niche Publishing Co., Bill Cory - 719-265-[   ] (fax[   ]); E-mail: Office is open 10 to 3 Pacific M—F. If you get "the machine," leave name, phone, & message. I will call you!
I welcome and would appreciate hearing all suggestions, comments and constructive criticism on our coverage, quality, and editorial approach, by email or phone!

Mail/Ship All Ad/Photo Materials Direct To This Address: or email ads to magads@mac.com

Wedding & Party Magazine, [   ]

" " " "PACKAGE ALL MATERIALS, ART & PHOTOS IN STIFF CORRUGATED CARDBOARD" " " "
If materials arrive damaged because of inadequate packaging, Publisher is not responsible or liable.

Information Form for FREE, NO-OBLIGATION LISTING of Reception Site in *Wedding & Party Magazine* <u>FAX to 719-</u>

Type of Establishment: Private Hall _____ Hotel _____ Private Residence _____

City/County Park _____ City/County Operated Hall _____ Bed & Breakfast _____

Other _____

EXACT NAME of Establishment As You Want It In Print: _____

_____

Address: _____

City, State, ZIP: _____

Phone: _____ Toll-Free Phone _____ Fax _____

E-Mail: _____ Web page _____

Person Filling Out This Form: _____ Phone_____

Owner or Manager Name: _____ Phone_____

Information on Banquet Rooms or Areas within Your Location:

Room/Area 1: Name _____ Capacity (Banquet Seating)_____

Room/Area 2: Name _____ Capacity (Banquet Seating) _____

Room/Area 2: Name _____ Capacity (Banquet Seating) _____

_____
Write in facts on your site, such as views, setting, kitchen facilities, dance floors or other items available, whether you assist with other services, etc. This form is for FACTS and FIGURES to help Brides decide.

_____

_____

_____

_____

_____

_____

_____

_____

_____

_____

<u>FAX to 719-</u>   . Thank you! THIS IS A <u>FREE</u> LISTING
Send a GOOD Photo of a Reception/Wedding in progress at your site and we'll use it!
Send photos to: Bill Cory,   .(or email: billcory@mac.com)

THANKS FOR USING <u>THIS FORM</u>; <u>NOT A BROCHURE or FACT SHEET</u>:

| Cour-
tesy of | | | | | | With a copy of this form at each phone; your
Staff can help your business grow! Small effort
will bring Profitable information! | | | | | |

CUSTOMER CALL SOURCE RECORD

X   Mark the appropriate columns beside each call.

| Ask Every Caller | "Would you mind telling me where you heard of us?" |

Multiple sources are common; experts say that many potential customers don't call until they "hear" your business name 3 times!

CALL DATE	Magazine Ad (which one?)	Newspaper Ad (which paper?)	Phone Book or Yellow Pgs	RADIO Ad (which Station?)	T.V. Ad (which Station?)	Referral from a Happy Customer or Business (name?)	Direct Mail	World Wide Web	Bridal Show (date?)	Othe
TOTALS										

THE WRITE-A-MAGAZINE CD PUBLISHING KIT

This set of resources will help you quickly to start your own publishing business. It will actually save you *weeks* of work in preparing your magazine layouts and previews.

I wish I had had a resource like this CD when I started! It would have prevented many, many headaches! The shortcuts I've discovered and used since 1990 are all provided as tools in the CD's files. Those techniques, now available to you, make it possible to prepare a 100+-page magazine for print in about three weeks! (And yes, that's working alone!)

What's on the CD? ...To start with, the complete systematic publishing methods I've used for twenty years are fully explained, with tools that were impossible to put into this book. It also includes all of the forms shown in this book, which you may use for guidance in creating your own forms. (*Please remember: I am not a lawyer, and the forms are not intended as legal documents; they are not intended to, and do not, constitute legal advice.*)

Then, to illustrate how a project progresses from a "preview edition" to a finished magazine, I've included the preview edition for a 40-page wedding publication, and the published magazine that resulted from it, with detailed annotations. In the notes on the PDF, I provide tips on how to make the magazine more effective and easier to create.

And since preview editions are *extremely* valuable in selling these magazine ads (especially for your very first one), I've included five Preview Editions in PDF so you can see how they flow. There are 40, 48, 56, 96 and 104-page previews. (If one of them fits your needs, you can simply add a cover, change some details, print and use it.)

Each of those preview editions led to published magazines. I've included nine published issues as PDFs, from 40 pages to 112 pages, from various years and locations, showing the evolution of the magazines with changes in ads, black-and-white to color interiors, etc. They have never been available until now, and I'm happy to offer them as guides.

And, then, there is the real heart of the CD, the graphic preview edition pages. I've discovered that one of the most troublesome tasks for a new publisher of these magazines is the creation of the preview editions. This CD solves that problem and makes it *so* easy, no matter which page layout program you use. Included are master pages — thirty of them — in TIF and EPS formats, with choices of an 8-per-page ad grid format or a 10-per-page ad grid format. From these grids, you can simply place the TIF or EPS ad grid on pages within any page layout program. Mix 'em up in any way you want; this is *your* magazine! It will streamline your production and get the preview edition done so your sales rep can get to work! Complete instructions are included.

Please see the next page for CD details and pricing.

CD CONTENTS:

Why Reinvent the Wheel?

The Contents of this CD will save you **weeks** *of time and make your publishing venture* <u>much</u> *easier!*

What's On The CD:

- Adobe InDesign® magazine files
- 48, 56, 96 and 104-page Preview Editions in Adobe PDF
- Complete Preview and the magazine it became, with notes.
- Nine complete published magazines in PDF: 40 to 112 pages
- Annotated versions of 40- and 112-page published magazines
- All forms illustrated and explained in this book
- TIF and EPS files with 8-per-page and 10-per page Masters
- Four printed magazines included with every order.

Save time and creative energy!

Get your publishing business started faster!

I've spent a full month putting onto this CD every tool I've used in the last 20 profitable years of publishing these small magazines. Its standard price is $159.95, but here's a great offer:

The printed version of the book is priced at $89.95 at Amazon and Lulu. (Total: $249.90 for both the CD and the printed book.)

But since you already have the book, *you get the CD for half price!*

Go to the link below to get the CD for just $79.95, including USPS Priority shipping!

Four recent printed magazines are included with every order!

Go to **www.WriteAMagazine.com** to order.

... What is your time worth?

email me with questions: ... WriteAMagazine@gmail.com

Made in the USA
Lexington, KY
11 July 2010